## DARK TOMORROW
### OFFICIAL STRATEGY GUIDE
By Bart Farkas

### CONTENTS

| | |
|---|---|
| Characters | 2 |
| Utility Belt & Hidden Items | 22 |
| Game Basics | 32 |
| **Walkthrough** | |
|    Prelude | 42 |
|    Gotham City Alleyway | 46 |
|    Gazette Square | 49 |
|    Warehouse District | 54 |
|    Gotham Docks | 60 |
|    Talbot Factory | 65 |
|    Underground Sewers | 69 |
|    Arkham Asylum | 75 |
|    Rā's al Ghūl's Castle | 92 |
| Secrets | 109 |

# CHARACTERS

# BATMAN

The legendary Dark Knight prowls the darkened streets of Gotham. The Caped Crusader strikes out at the heart of evil, and no city has a darker heart. Donned in a high-tech, bullet-resistant, flexible armor complete with bat-shaped cowl, Batman fights crime with an arsenal of advanced gadgetry and superior martial arts skills. Attacking criminals from the shadows, Batman uses cunning and skill to topple common thieves and armed thugs.

Batman refuses to use guns, due to the trauma he endured at a young age by his alter ego, Bruce Wayne. As a boy, Thomas and Martha Wayne took him to see a movie. Upon leaving the theater, the family attempted to take a shortcut through Gotham's heinous side streets, dubbed "Crime Alley." The family was mugged and Bruce's parents were fatally shot. The robber escaped and was never caught. As he watched his mother and father pass away in that dark alleyway, the young boy vowed that no criminal would ever go unpunished again.

Young Bruce inherited his father's fortune and company. Although a board of executives assumed temporary leadership of the Wayne Enterprises, Bruce was entrusted to the family butler, Alfred Pennyworth. The lifelong family servant could sense the repressed rage in young Bruce, and guided the child to direct his aggression in positive directions.

Bruce studied abroad for most of his childhood, and spent a good deal of time in Japan. He dreamed of returning to the streets of Gotham and exerting vigilante justice with his own hands. Because of his intense hatred of firearms, he swore to stop criminals without using guns. For several years, he studied the legendary martial arts of Japan's mythic ninja warriors, who used disguises and struck their opponents from the shadows.

Learning the stealth and techniques of the ninja, Batman returned to Wayne Manor following his graduation from college. On his 21st birthday, Bruce assumed the presidency of Wayne Enterprises and utilized his company's vast technological resources to develop high-power stealth weaponry and gadgets to use to fight crime. With Alfred's help, he transformed the ancient bat caves under Wayne Manor into a crime-fighting headquarters. The Batcave is now home to a giant super computer, which enables Batman to monitor and access all criminal and defense records. Any time crime occurs in Gotham City, Batman is there.

| Real Name | Bruce Wayne |
| --- | --- |
| Occupation | Industrialist, Philanthropist |
| Base of Operations | Gotham City |
| Marital Status | Single |
| Height | 6' 2" |
| Weight | 210 |
| Eyes | Blue |
| Hair | Black |
| First Appearance | DETECTIVE COMICS #27 (May, 1939) |

# CHARACTERS

# ALFRED

Alfred Pennyworth is the consummate gentleman's gentleman and the loyal servant of the Wayne family since his departure from acting with the Royal Shakespeare Company of England. Following the deaths of Thomas and Martha Wayne, Alfred was left in charge of the young billionaire. The butler soon learned that the boy was harboring a deep obsession with criminals, and a burning desire to somehow avenge his parents' deaths. Identifying the rage within young Master Wayne, Alfred attempted to guide Bruce on a more civilized, humanitarian path to seeking justice.

Under Alfred's tutelage, Bruce traveled abroad to study and learned the mechanics of engineering as well as advanced martial arts. Recalling his acting skills of yesteryear, Alfred taught Bruce the art of vocal mimicry and theatrical makeup, since any proper vigilante should be wise enough to use a disguise.

Serving in many ways as Bruce's surrogate father, Alfred has become the most trusted ally and confidant of both Bruce Wayne and his alter ego, Batman. Night after night, as Batman hunts criminals, Alfred waits patiently for Bruce Wayne to return home. He tends to whatever wounds the crime fighter suffers, and adopts an air of resigned tolerance toward Batman's pursuits. Alfred attempts to remind his young master that he is still human, and voices his fatherly concerns for Bruce's safety.

| Real Name | Alfred Pennyworth |
|---|---|
| Occupation | Butler |
| Base of Operations | Wayne Manor, Gotham City |
| Marital Status | Single |
| Height | 6' 0" |
| Weight | 160 |
| Eyes | Blue |
| Hair | Black |
| First Appearance | BATMAN #16 (April-May, 1943) |

# ORACLE

Like Bruce Wayne, Barbara Gordon has also experienced tragedy in her life. Both of her parents died in a horrific car crash, forcing her to live in Gotham City with her Uncle James Gordon and his wife. When Barbara dressed up like a female version of Batman for a costume party, she had no idea that she would end up saving billionaire Bruce Wayne from Killer Moth. The Dark Knight asked her to join his crusade not long thereafter, but Barbara's lack of combat training often placed her in tight spots against the arch-criminals. When the Joker discovered her true identity he shot her at her own house, paralyzing her for life.

Although her career as a crime fighter is over, Barbara continues to aid Batman in his quest for justice. Barbara has a photographic memory, and through her position as Gotham Library Administrator she has access to scores of the world's top newspapers and magazines. She can instantly recall factual information from any source. Through WayneTech financing, Barbara has assembled an extremely complex and powerful computer system with unmatched network capabilities. Utilizing her technical savvy, Barbara can access sources such as the CIA's mainframe, as well as the private servers of the FBI, NSA, and Interpol. With incredible hacking skills in an information technology age, Barbara has adopted the codename "Oracle" and continues to be of assistance to Batman in his crusades against crime.

Production Images

| | |
|---|---|
| **Real Name** | Barbara Gordon |
| **Occupation** | Library Administrator |
| **Base of Operations** | Gotham City |
| **Marital Status** | Single |
| **Height** | 5' 11" |
| **Weight** | 126 |
| **Eyes** | Blue |
| **Hair** | Red |
| **First Appearance** | (As Batgirl) DETECTIVE COMICS #359 (January, 1967)<br>(As Oracle) SUICIDE SQUAD #23 (January, 1989) |

# CHARACTERS

# COMMISSIONER GORDON

As Commissioner of the Gotham City Police Department, James Gordon often walks a fine line between moral dilemmas. Since his transfer to the department from Chicago, he has been tasked to subdue police corruption in his own department whilst attempting to apprehend the most violent and diabolical criminals history has ever known. Jim is forced to place his marriage and his family in harm's way to pursue what he knows is right. In spite of political roadblocks and bureaucratic stalling, Gordon has amassed an amazing record of arrests and convictions. There was no longer any way to publicly justify *not* appointing him to the Commissioner's seat. Not long after his promotion, he was given one simple order: To arrest the mysterious vigilante known only as "The Batman."

In spite of his assignment, Gordon could not turn a blind eye to the fact that he was hunting an individual who sought to bring criminals to justice, much like himself. Although Gordon feels that vigilante actions are just a step below total anarchy, he also realizes that Batman is passionate for justice. Gordon figures that if Batman has the will, the resources, and the abilities to take down criminals when the hands of the police are tied, then it is better to join the Dark Knight in his crusade rather than fight him.

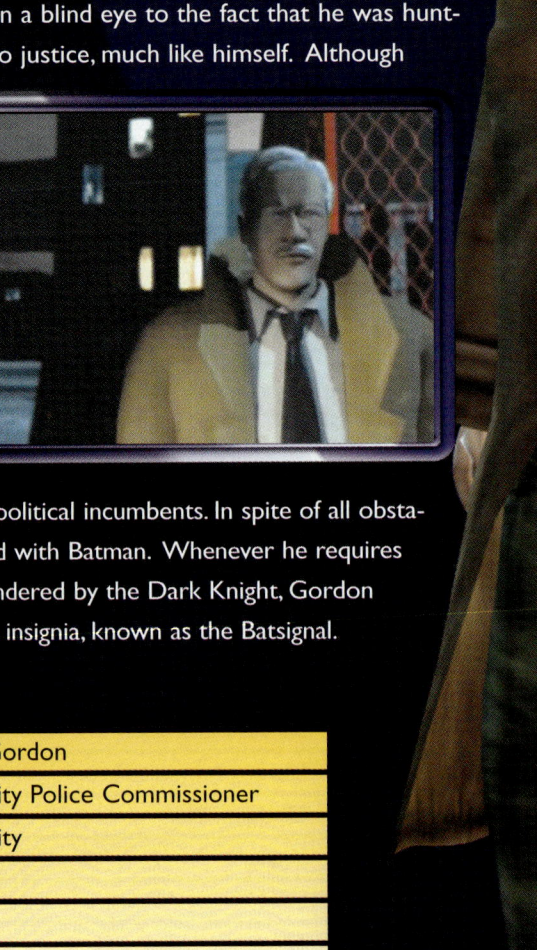

The two men have formed an uneasy alliance, which is often disturbed by the machinations of criminal masterminds as well as political incumbents. In spite of all obstacles, however, Commissioner Gordon has bonded with Batman. Whenever he requires the kind of special assistance that can only be rendered by the Dark Knight, Gordon switches on a large spotlight fitted with Batman's insignia, known as the Batsignal.

| Real Name | James W. Gordon |
|---|---|
| Occupation | Gotham City Police Commissioner |
| Base of Operations | Gotham City |
| Marital Status | Widower |
| Height | 5' 9" |
| Weight | 168 |
| Eyes | Blue |
| Hair | Formerly brown, now white |
| First Appearance | DETECTIVE COMICS #27 (May, 1939) |

# ROBIN

When criminals murdered Dick Grayson's acrobat family, he was adopted as the ward of billionaire Bruce Wayne. Soon after he learned of his guardian's true identity, and Batman had a partner in crime fighting. The Boy Wonder known as Robin soon became an essential balance for Batman's insatiable thirst for vengeance and justice. However, as Dick grew older he could no longer subdue the darker side of Batman, and he left the Dark Knight to fight alone once again. Batman hastily accepted a new Robin, Jason Todd. However, Jason soon proved that his anger and frustration with crime was too similar to Batman's. His reckless behavior caused him to fall into a trap, leading to Todd's murder by The Joker.

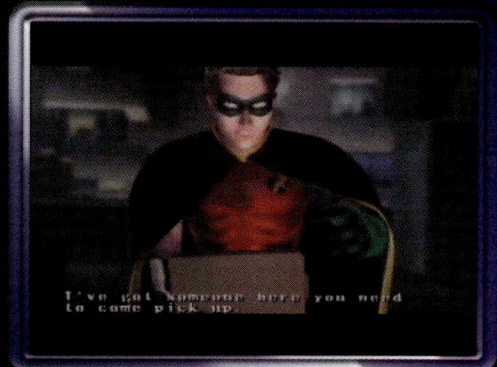

After fighting crime on his own for a long time, Batman felt he could no longer go on without a Robin. Circumstances brought him together with a young man named Timothy Drake, whose parents had also met with an untimely fate at the hands of criminals. Although Tim bears the same burden as Bruce, his maturity and wisdom allow him to cope with his issues more thoroughly. Because of the mistakes Batman feels he made with past Robins, he rarely involves the young man directly in any of his investigations. Robin is often assigned to surveillance and reconnaissance work. Although Tim Drake feels proud and justified in his role as Robin, his combat skills are nowhere near the level required to take on archfiends such as Mr. Freeze or The Joker.

| Real Name | Timothy Drake |
|---|---|
| Occupation | High School Student |
| Base of Operations | Gotham City |
| Marital Status | Single |
| Height | 5' 1" |
| Weight | 115 |
| Eyes | Blue |
| Hair | Black |
| First Appearance | (As Tim Drake) BATMAN #436 (August, 1989) (As Robin) BATMAN #457 (December, 1990) |

# CHARACTERS

# BATGIRL

In spite of the fact that she couldn't read or speak, this dependable young woman impressed Barbara Gordon. The main reason probably had something to do with the fact that Cassandra saved Barbara's uncle, Commissioner Gordon, from death at the hands of the world's most dangerous assassin. Following this faithful deed, Barbara recommended that Batman take the young girl under his wing, as the new Batgirl. Only later did Barbara learn that the assassin Cassandra had thwarted was her very own father, David Cain.

From an early age, Cassandra's father instructed her in every possible form of combat. Her mastery of the deadly arts is so deep that she outranks even Batman himself. She could be quite possibly the most dangerous martial artist in the world. Her disposition and willingness to pursue justice even against her own father result from an incident in her early years, where she inadvertently assassinated an innocent man. Silently, she quests for justice and peace in an attempt to atone for her unbearable mistake.

| Real Name | Cassandra Cain |
|---|---|
| Occupation | Costumed Adventurer |
| Base of Operations | Gotham City |
| Marital Status | Single |
| Height | 5"5" |
| Weight | 110 |
| Eyes | Brown |
| Hair | Black |
| First Appearance | BATMAN #567 (July 1999) |

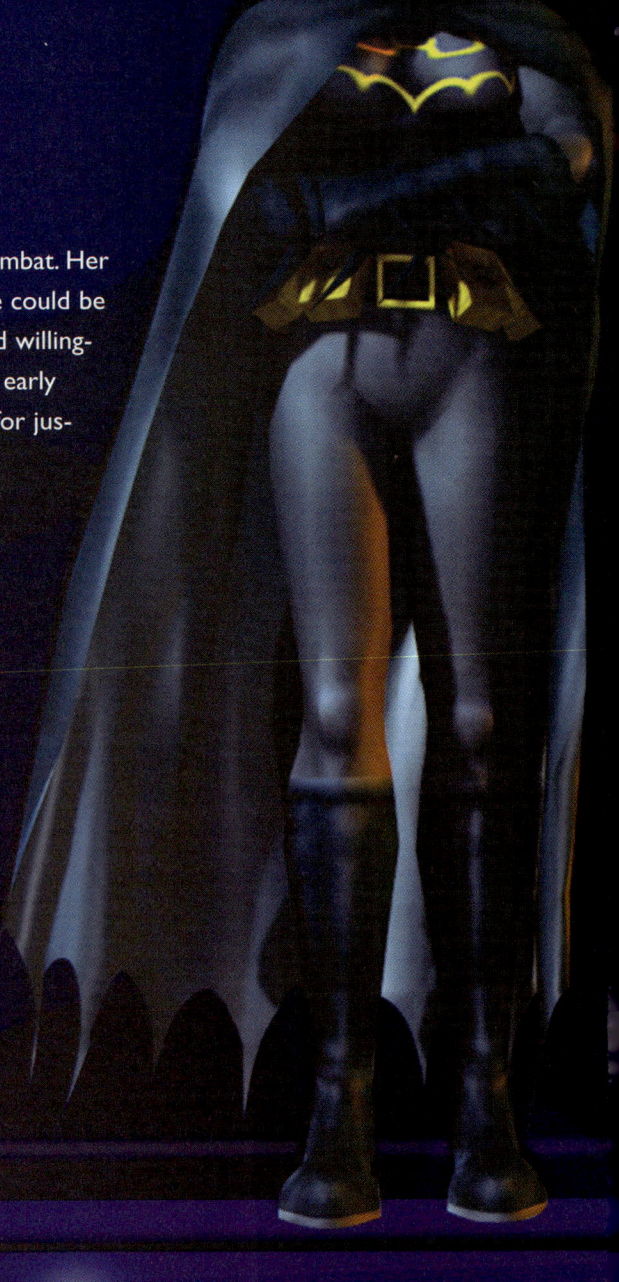

# DR. ARKHAM

As the descendent of Amadeus Arkham, the founder of Arkham Asylum, Jeremiah is a man who upholds a proud family history of mental patient treatment. However, he must also maintain the horrible secret of his ancestors—that insanity runs in his bloodline! Sometimes, his interest in the delusions and ravings of his patients runs deeper than he should allow. On the outside, though, Dr. Arkham maintains the calm and dependable demeanor most people expect of an esteemed administrator. Dr. Arkham has been a reliable source of information on escaped mental patients, whenever Batman or the police are trying to track them down.

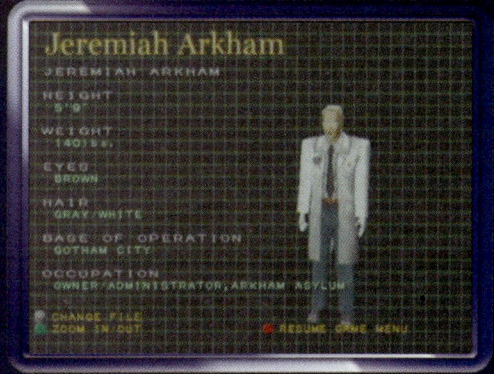

| Real Name | Jeremiah Arkham, M.D. |
| --- | --- |
| Occupation | Owner/Administrator, Arkham Asylum |
| Base of Operations | Gotham City |
| Marital Status | Married |
| Height | 5' 9" |
| Weight | 140 |
| Eyes | Brown |
| Hair | Gray/White |
| First Appearance | BATMAN: SHADOW OF THE BAT #1 |

# CHARACTERS

# LT. BULLOCK

This hard-nosed, cynical detective doesn't share Commissioner Gordon's bond with "The Bat" but he knows that Gordon values the vigilante's assistance on big cases. His respect and admiration for the Commissioner is probably what keeps Bullock from going after Batman any chance he gets.

| | |
|---|---|
| Real Name | Harvey Bullock |
| Occupation | Detective Lieutenant, GCPD |
| Base of Operations | Gotham City |
| Marital Status | Single |
| Height | 5' 10" |
| Weight | 250 |
| Eyes | Brown |
| Hair | Brown |
| First Appearance | BATMAN #361 (July 1983) |

# LT. MONTOYA

Montoya is Lt. Bullock's levelheaded partner, who quite often keeps the impatient detective out of trouble. She shares Bullock's respect for Commissioner Gordon, but not his dislike for Batman—although sometimes she wonders if Gordon doesn't rely on the Dark Knight a little too much.

| | |
|---|---|
| Real Name | Renee Montoya |
| Occupation | Detective Lieutenant, GCPD |
| Base of Operations | Gotham City |
| Marital Status | Single |
| Height | 5' 6" |
| Weight | 125 |
| Eyes | Brown |
| Hair | Brown |
| First Appearance | BATMAN #361 (July 1983) |

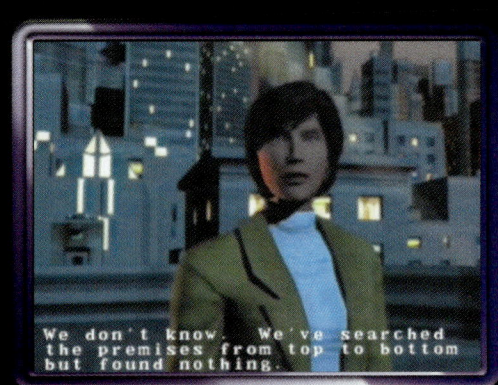

# BLACK MASK

Heir to the Janus Cosmetics fortune, Roman Sionis may have been mentally unstable since infancy. The rich and powerful Sionis family was acquainted with the Wayne family. When Roman and Bruce Wayne were young boys, they didn't always get along because Roman was so distant. Roman's secret interests rest in setting fires and torturing helpless animals.

As a young man, Roman began dating the spokesmodel for Janus Cosmetics. When his parents voiced their disapproval, they suspiciously died soon thereafter in a fire. Roman inherited the family company, married the model and obsessively collected expensive masks. His collection ranged from important archaeological relics to cheap, plastic Halloween masks.

Roman's downfall began when he announced that his company would release a new line of foundations for men and women named "Facepaint." The product was designed to cover a person's face, much like a mask. The project failed and his company's stock began to plummet. Janus quickly released a new line of products, which claimed to be completely waterproof. Because of the ineffectual testing of the makeup, many customers were scarred for life. As his company headed for financial ruin, Roman accepted a buyout offer from Wayne Enterprises. The deal included the appointment of WayneTech executives to the highest positions in the company. Roman was ousted.

No longer wealthy, Roman was abandoned by his supermodel wife. Retreating to his family crypt, he chopped a piece from his father's casket. He eventually fashioned the piece into the Black Mask, which he wore as he gathered an army of criminals and plotted revenge. He began abducting and murdering the WayneTech executives in charge of his company. In a climactic battle with Batman, the Black Mask was burned permanently onto Roman's face. In Roman's psychosis, he believed the Black Mask had claimed him, body and soul. He *became* the mask.

| Real Name | Roman Sionis |
|---|---|
| Occupation | Crime Lord |
| Base of Operations | Gotham City |
| Marital Status | Single |
| Height | 6' 1" |
| Weight | 195 |
| Eyes | Brown |
| Hair | Brown |
| First Appearance | BATMAN #386 (August, 1985) |

# CHARACTERS

# SCARFACE AND THE VENTRILOQUIST

Arnold Wesker was a mild-mannered ventriloquist, but his act wasn't getting any applause. When his wife took all of his money and disappeared, Arnold experienced a psychological schism that may have split his personality in half.

Although Arnold seems to remain perfectly timid and fearful, his vicious sub-personality exhibits itself through his puppet, Scarface. Adopting the personality of a prohibition-era gangster, Scarface is lewd, violent-tempered and deadly. While Scarface organizes gangs, orders drug shipments and plots heist capers, Arnold Wesker can only register his meek complaints and objections to what is occurring. Due to Arnold's weakness, Scarface often refers to Arnold as his "dummy." When confronting Batman, Scarface is determined to go out guns blazing, despite Arnold's frightened, remorseful protests. Although he pities Arnold's dilemma, Batman never hesitates to enforce justice.

| | |
|---|---|
| **Real Name** | Arnold Wesker |
| **Occupation** | Crime Lord |
| **Base of Operations** | Gotham City |
| **Marital Status** | Divorced |
| **Height** | 5' 7" |
| **Weight** | 142 |
| **Eyes** | Unrevealed |
| **Hair** | Gray |
| **First Appearance** | DETECTIVE COMICS #583 (February, 1988) |

# RATCATCHER

Otis Flannegan was an employee of Gotham City's Sanitation Department, assigned to subdue the overwhelming rodent population. The rats stopped surfacing within the city, but Otis was never heard from again. He was assumed dead until he reappeared quite suddenly during the commuter train rescue attempt. Otis had developed a predatory obsession with the rats he was assigned to exterminate, and the depth of his psychosis caused him to believe that rats are a superior species to mankind. He intended for the innocent civilians trapped on the wrecked train to provide an excellent lunch for his new pets.

Utilizing bizarre and disturbing interspecies breeding techniques, Flannegan breeds gigantic rats and trains them to attack humans. His extensive knowledge of the Gotham City sewer systems has enabled Otis to escape capture on several occasions, even from high-security facilities such as Stonewall prison and Arkham Asylum. While Otis is no match for the combat prowess of Batman, his mutant rodent friends will fight to the grizzly death to protect their beloved master.

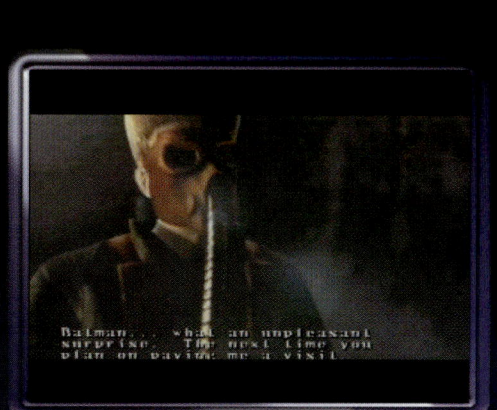

| Real Name | Otis Flannegan |
|---|---|
| Occupation | Professional Criminal |
| Base of Operations | Sewers Below Gotham City |
| Marital Status | Single |
| Height | 5' 10" |
| Weight | 160 |
| Eyes | Blue |
| Hair | Blonde |
| First Appearance | BATMAN #555 (June, 1998) |

# CHARACTERS

# MR. FREEZE

Victor Fries was a well respected scientist, biochemist, and engineer. His company was purchased by Wayne Enterprises, which gave him access to virtually unlimited sources of funding. His work on cryogenics and the preservation of living tissue through freezing brought Victor a certain amount of renown, and the invitations to Gotham's high society events started pouring in. It could be said that Victor was the happiest man on earth, but he was most happy with his beautiful and intelligent wife Nora.

The tragedy of Victor's life began when Nora developed a rare genetic disease. Unwilling to lose his beloved wife, Victor used his research facilities to cryogenically freeze Nora until a cure could be found. He then devoted all of his funding and work to curing her disease, but all of the research and experiments failed. His staff resigned, and conditions in the cryogenics lab became unstable and hazardous.

Although it saddened Bruce Wayne to do so, he was forced to cancel Victor's contract and revoke his funding. While Bruce hoped that his friend could finally allow Nora to die, Victor refused. He attempted to conduct further experiments, hastily and without the required safety precautions. An accident occurred and Victor was caught in a blast of pure coolant. Strangely, the chemicals he was mixing at the time allowed him to stay alive, while his body temperature was permanently lowered to an unnatural degree. As a result, Victor could not endure room temperature, only deadly, subzero conditions. He constructed a special suit, which maintains his body at the proper temperature at all times.

This unfortunate incident also affected Victor's mind so that he no longer felt human emotions or compassion.

Obsessed with his dilemma, he stole his wife's body and stored her in an unknown location. Victor continues to conduct his unsanctioned experiments to cure her affliction, and funds his own research through brilliantly staged crimes and robberies. He uses his knowledge of coolants and freezing methods to create weapons that can flash-freeze humans on contact. Cold of heart and void of humanity, Victor sees no reason why anyone should be happy.

| Real Name | Victor Fries |
|---|---|
| Occupation | Professional Criminal |
| Base of Operations | Gotham City |
| Marital Status | Married |
| Height | 6' 0" |
| Weight | 190 |
| Eyes | Blue |
| Hair | White |
| First Appearance | BATMAN #121 (February, 1959) |

# ZSASZ

Victor Zsasz is a homicidal maniac the likes of which Gotham has never seen before. After gambling away his family fortune, he wandered the streets for hours until, ironically, a man tried to mug him. Zsasz overpowered and murdered the assailant. The bitter stupidity of the incident caused Zsasz to reach the conclusion that the human condition was ridiculous and life was meaningless.

Zsasz then embarked on one of the longest serial killing sprees in recorded history, carving a slash in his body for each of his victims. He made 140 marks before his capture and subsequent incarceration. Zsasz bides his time in an asylum, toying with poor Dr. Arkham and waiting for a chance to escape.

| Real Name | Victor Zsasz |
|---|---|
| Occupation | Professional Criminal |
| Base of Operations | Gotham City |
| Marital Status | Single |
| Height | 5' 10" |
| Weight | 155 |
| Eyes | Blue |
| Hair | Blonde |
| First Appearance | BATMAN: SHADOW OF THE BAT #1 (June, 1992) |

# CHARACTERS

# KILLER CROC

Waylon Jones is afflicted with a bizarre genetic disorder that slowly mutates his DNA, making him look like a human crocodile. Because of his condition, the only way he could make a living was to become a professional wrestler, "Killer Croc." But after conflicts with management, he quit. Croc now uses his brute strength for criminal purposes. He can break through reinforced steel doors, such as those used for bank vaults.

Batman is no match for Killer Croc's immense physical power. But as Waylon's appearance becomes more and more reptilian, his mental faculties decay as well. Batman must outsmart Killer Croc during each of their encounters, instead of relying on hand-to-hand combat.

| Real Name | Waylon Jones |
|---|---|
| Occupation | Former Alligator Wrestler, Pro Criminal |
| Base of Operations | Gotham City |
| Marital Status | Single |
| Height | 6' 5" |
| Weight | 268 |
| Eyes | Red |
| Hair | None |
| First Appearance | BATMAN #357 (January, 1994) |

# POISON IVY

The seeds of Pamela Isley's demise were sown under the tutelage of Jason Woodrue, a.k.a. the Floronic Man. During an experiment in plant/animal hybridization, Woodrue transformed the unwilling Isley into a beautiful creature whose veins pumped toxins. Her skin now exudes pheromones that drive men wild.

To support her own botanical experiments and extravagant lifestyle, Isley began a life of crime. Naturally, she gravitated to the dark and chaotic Gotham City. This is where she encountered Batman, who developed an anti-toxin for himself to resist her otherworldly charms. Because he is the one man who cannot fall under her spell, Poison Ivy has developed an obsession with Batman. She is always looking for a way to make him fall in love with her.

| Real Name | Pamela Lillian Isley |
|---|---|
| Occupation | Professional Criminal |
| Base of Operations | Gotham City |
| Marital Status | Single |
| Height | 5'6" |
| Weight | 110 |
| Eyes | Green |
| Hair | Chestnut |
| First Appearance | BATMAN #181 (June, 1966) |

# CHARACTERS

# THE JOKER

The first and most fearsome of all of Batman's opponents is this diabolical mastermind of chaos, the supreme arch villain by which all others pale in comparison. So deep are the layers of his twisted personality that no one can ascertain his true identity, what caused his skin to become such a shocking white color, or why his mouth is perpetually frozen in a maniacal grimace of evil and sadistic delight.

However, there is one thing that no one doubts: the Joker is the most dangerous individual alive. His sole design is to murder and destroy, preferably in mass quantities. Although some of his capers involve robbery and extortion, the vast majority of the Joker's plans involve local or global destruction of the general populace.

In all of his insane actions, no matter how illogically constructed or self-destructive they turn out to be, the Joker seems to have one purpose in mind: to attract the attention of Batman, against whom he harbors some unspoken grudge. The Dark Knight watches and waits, dreading the day that the Joker might once again escape the confines of Arkham Asylum. But Batman remains ready, nonetheless.

| | |
|---|---|
| **Real Name** | Unknown |
| **Occupation** | Professional Criminal |
| **Base of Operations** | Gotham City |
| **Marital Status** | Single |
| **Height** | 6' 5" |
| **Weight** | 192 |
| **Eyes** | Green |
| **Hair** | Green |
| **First Appearance** | BATMAN #1 (Spring, 1940) |

# RĀ'S AL GHŪL

The man known as Rā's al Ghūl (Arabic for "The Demon's Head) is as much a mystery as Batman's true identity is to the citizens of Gotham. An apocalyptic figure, he masterfully plots world domination by engineering cataclysms and plague. With mankind facing extinction, he plans to rise as the new messiah. Although every bit as contemptuous of humankind as the Joker, his ironclad schemes denote a fierce intelligence and a logical methodology that even Batman must respect.

Rā's al Ghūl first contacted Batman in the guise of an ally, luring him to the Middle East to help him uncover a group of global terrorists and rescue his kidnapped daughter. The Dark Knight soon learned that the organization was headed by the Demon's Head himself. Thereafter, it was revealed that Rā's al Ghūl was centuries old, extending his life by utilizing the strange power of his ancient "Lazarus Pits." However, the effect of the pits cannot extend one's life to immortality and Rā's life force is waning.

Rā's al Ghūl considers Batman his only worthy living opponent, and for that reason he wishes for him to marry his gorgeous daughter Talia and inherit the evil empire. Considering the instant bond he felt with Talia, Batman is still deeply torn between his feelings and his lifelong mission. However, Batman's laser-like focus on justice prevailed, and Rā's has been his enemy ever since.

| Real Name | Unknown |
| --- | --- |
| Occupation | International Terrorist |
| Base of Operations | Mobile |
| Marital Status | Single |
| Height | 6' 5" |
| Weight | 215 |
| Eyes | Green |
| Hair | Gray with white streaks |
| First Appearance | BATMAN #232 (June, 1971) |

# CHARACTERS

# TALIA

The daughter of Rā's al Ghūl, Talia's past and true age are unknown. In his old-world thinking, Rā's would never consider letting a woman inherit his empire. However, this does not diminish Talia's intense love and admiration for her father. She believes firmly in his quest to purify the planet, to destroy mankind before they can destroy themselves.

Not once did Talia question her father's thinking or beliefs until she met Bruce Wayne, whom she knows also as Batman. Growing up under the oppressive circumstances of her father's lifestyle, she is perhaps the one person who truly understands the duality of Bruce's nature. As a result, Talia loves both Bruce and Batman fiercely, and has begun to argue with her father as a result. Batman can't predict whether Talia will side with him, or aid her father in his quest to eliminate the "pestilence" of mankind. Talia feels the weight of her conflicted loyalties, but she still cannot be fully trusted.

| Real Name | Talia |
| --- | --- |
| Occupation | Adventurer, International Terrorist |
| Base of Operations | Mobile |
| Marital Status | Single |
| Height | 5' 8" |
| Weight | 120 |
| Eyes | Green |
| Hair | Brown |
| First Appearance | DETECTIVE COMICS #411 (May, 1971) |

# UBU

Rā's al Ghūl is never without the intimidating presence of his most trusted bodyguard, Ubu. This massive mound of muscle is a physical match for Batman, whom Ubu refers to as "infidel" for disrespecting the wishes of Rā's al Ghūl. Ubu's weapons training and hand-to-hand combat skills are on a similar level to Batman's. The only difference is that Ubu has been trained in the desert form of martial arts. Just as Rā's al Ghūl has reappeared time and again after Batman thought he was dead, so too has Ubu returned from certain demise on more than one occasion. Perhaps he too reaps some benefit from the rejuvenating Lazarus Pits.

| Real Name | Ubu |
|---|---|
| Occupation | Bodyguard of Rā's al Ghūl |
| Base of Operations | Mobile |
| Marital Status | Single |
| Height | 7' 0" |
| Weight | 300 |
| Eyes | Brown |
| Hair | None |
| First Appearance | BATMAN #232, June 1971 |

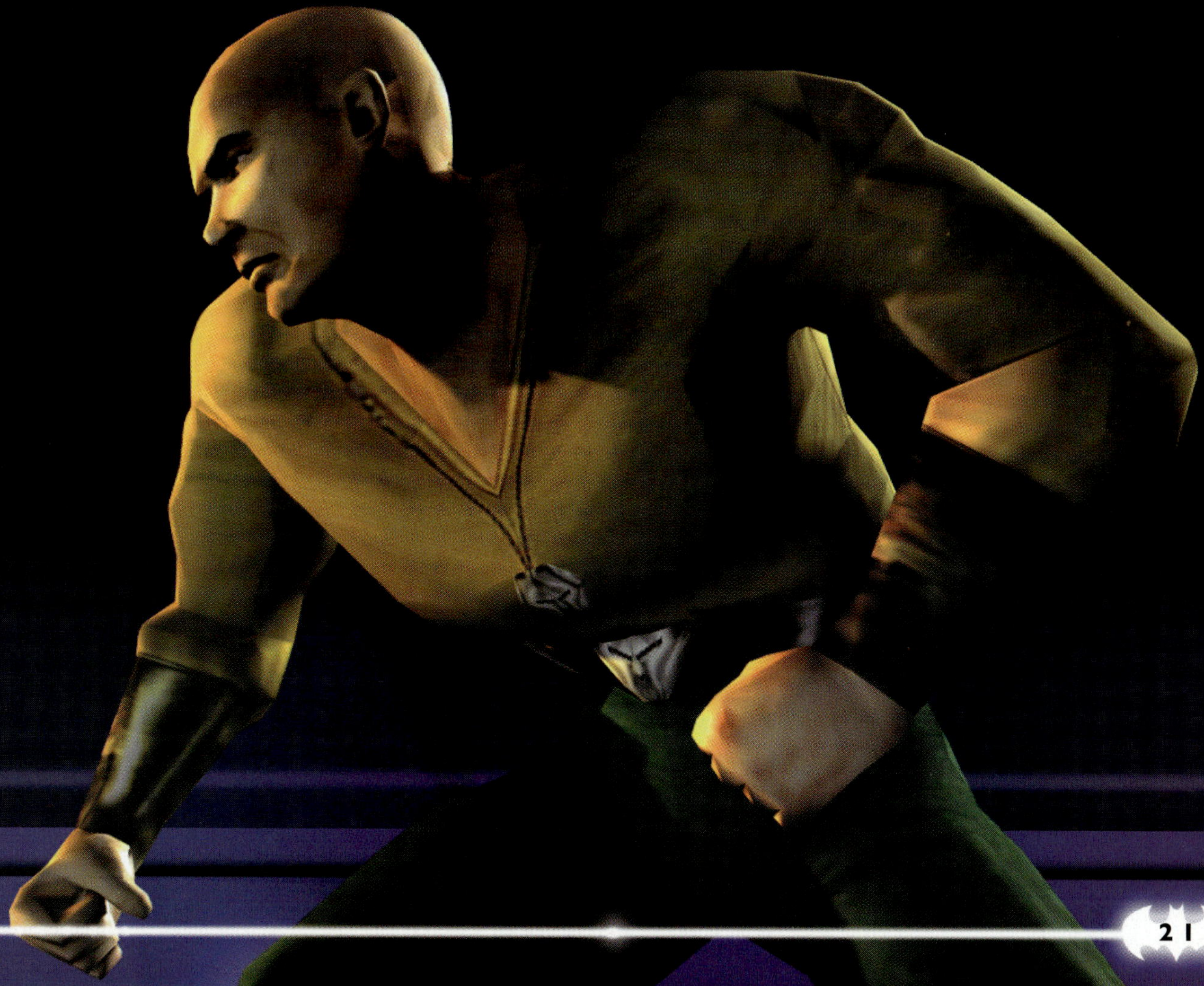

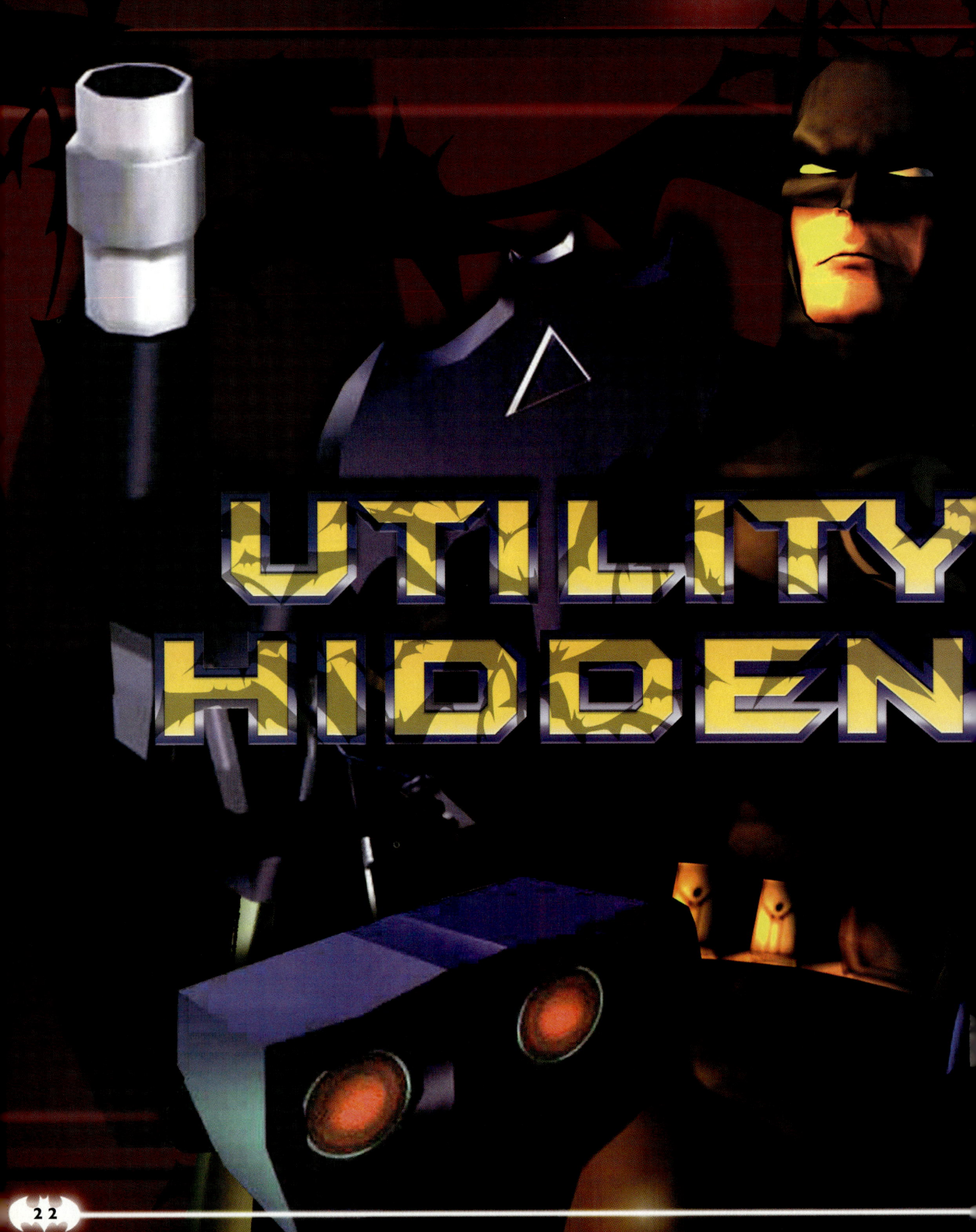

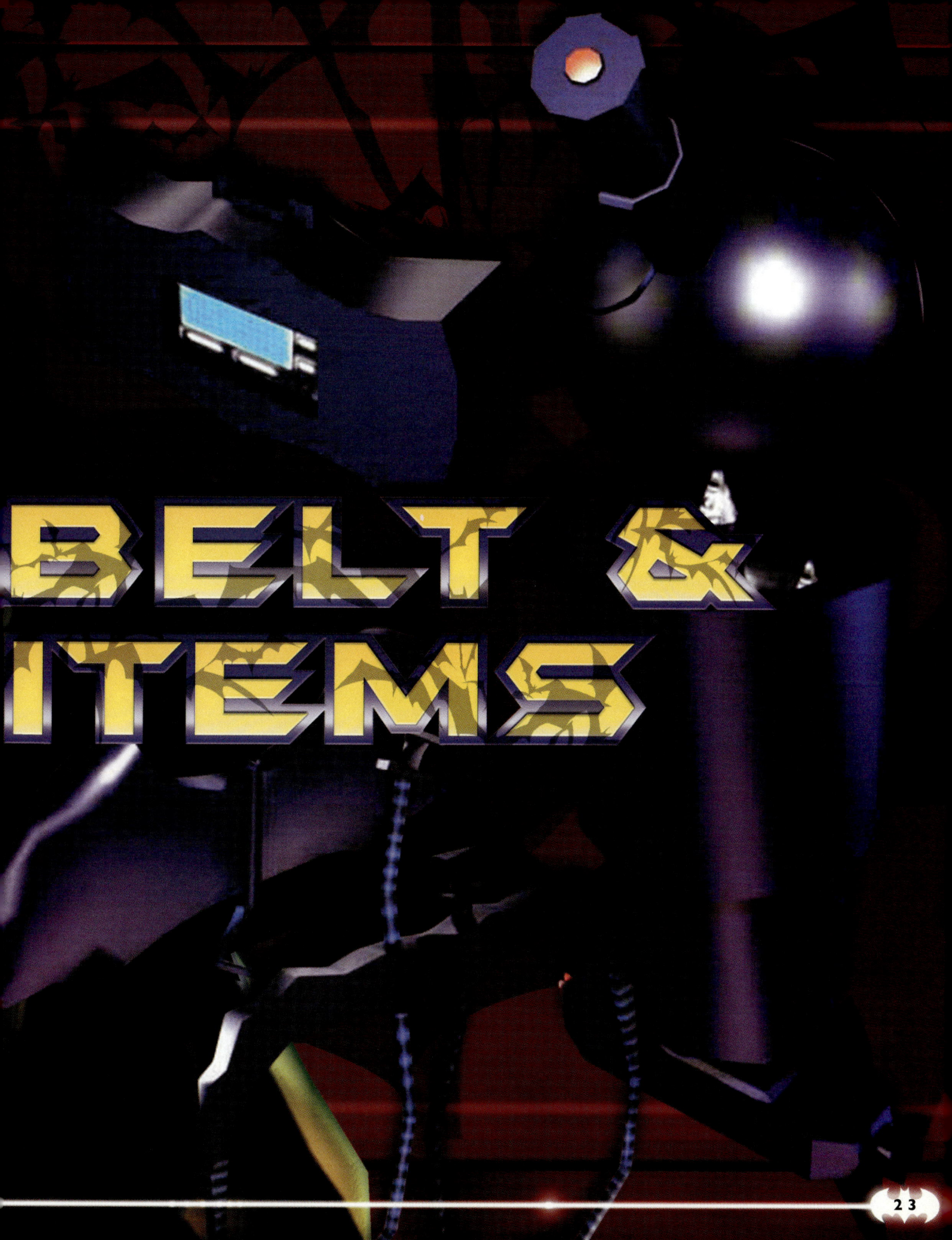

# BELT & ITEMS

# UTILITY BELT

Familiarize yourself with the functions and usage of Batman's gadgetry, plus the various items that he can pick up during the missions. Mastery of these devices will take practice, so allow yourself some time to experiment with them, mess up a few times, and maybe even fall off a few buildings. But also, learn from your mistakes and try something different the next time!

This section details the basic functions of Batman's handy little devices. For more in-depth information on how to use these items to neutralize the bad guys and save the day, refer to the chapter called "Game Basics."

## BATGEAR

Batman starts each game with a supply of his trademark gizmos stocked on the famous Bat Utility Belt. If Batman succumbs to the bad guys and you continue your game, you can select three different gear deployment types. The options follow:

1. **Offensive:** Batarangs (x20), Smoke Capsules (x5), Small Medical Kit. This deployment allows for greater aggression when fighting from a distance.
2. **Defensive:** Batarangs (x10), Smoke Capsules (x5), Large Medical Kit. This is a good choice for beginning players, or folks who like to take down crime with hand-to-hand combat. You'll need to recover often!
3. **Stealth:** Batarangs (x10), Smoke Capsules (x10), Small Medical Kit. This deployment enables Batman to create more diversions or obscure an enemy's vision while he sneaks past.

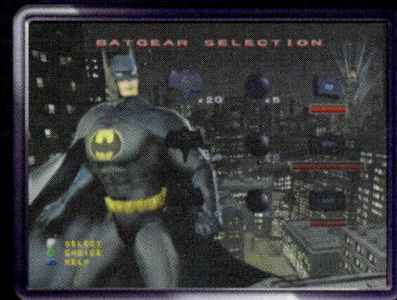

## BATCUFFS

These special wrist binders are made of highly compressed military material developed secretly at WayneTech. A diamond-edged cutting tool is needed to remove them.

The Batcuffs are probably the most important, and most used, item in Batman's arsenal. Because Batman refuses to use firearms, most of his methods only serve to stun an enemy. Those foes who get knocked down will recover shortly, and they will search for the person who tagged them. By using the Batcuffs when the hoodlum is down, the enemy will be rendered immobile and inoperative.

To use the Batcuffs on a prone enemy, stand very close to the body. Press left or right on the Directional Pad until the Batcuffs are selected, and press the Use button to apply them to the criminal. There is an easier way to apply the Batcuffs without having to cycle through the rest of the Batgear. Simply use the Quick Restraint button. Batman has an unlimited number of Batcuffs.

## FINGERLIGHT

The Fingerlight is basically a small light that can be used to illuminate dark areas. Select the Fingerlight in the lower-left portion of the screen, and press the Use button to equip it. Rotate the Analog Stick to shine the light on surrounding surfaces. While the Fingerlight is in use, Batman automatically enters Sneak mode, so movement is slowed considerably. Batman can also crouch while utilizing the Fingerlight. Because Nightvision won't work in black areas that are completely devoid of light, rely on this small light to get through. The special battery that powers the device makes this a flashlight that never goes out!

## NIGHTVISION

Starlite nightvision lenses are built into Batman's cowl and with the attachment of a small device these lenses can illuminate dim areas that are not completely devoid of light. Nightvision lenses enable Batman to see in poorly lit or cramped areas, and they will also reveal the locations of hidden laser beams and other traps. Nightvision can be used to enter First-Person View.

## UNIVERSAL TOOL

In general, the Universal Tool is a lock-picking device that opens some locked doors encountered in the game. While exploring the burrows and haunts of known criminals, try the Universal Tool on locked doors. You may just find secret areas with useful items inside!

The Universal Tool is also used during certain events and sequences to record incriminating conversations.

## BATGRAPPLE

The Bat Grapple uses a special CO2 cartridge to fire a grappling hook connected to a cable at least 200 feet straight up. Once the Bat Grapple is secured to an overhead surface, such as a roof or catwalk, Batman will launch upward.

Smoke Capsules and Batarangs can be used to surprise enemies while hanging from the cable. To make Batman face in any direction, rotate the Analog Stick. When the Analog Stick is pressed in the direction of Batman's back while the Jump button is pressed simultaneously, he will swing backwards and dismount, flying forward a short distance. You must master this maneuver to make proper use of the Bat Grapple.

## BATARANG

Batman's signature throwing devices have rounded edges and curved, aerodynamic, bat-shaped metal pieces. To enhance his throwing ability, there is a targeting system built into the lenses of Batman's cowl. The Batarangs are thermodynamically programmed to assist in reaching the intended target.

When the Batarang is selected on the utility belt, press the Use button to enter First-Person Aim mode. Line up the sighting on the intended target. When the crosshairs change to the shape of the bat symbol, press the Punch button to throw it. A successful toss with the Batarang usually knocks a foe unconscious for a short period of time.

You can even throw Batarangs at inanimate, non-living objects to cause a distraction. Throw them at barrels full of fuel or combustible material to create an explosion that will incapacitate multiple foes at once. When a Batarang strikes a wall or inanimate object at a reasonably close range, it can be picked up and used again. However, if a Batarang is used to knock someone down or blow up a barrel, it cannot be used again.

# UTILITY BELT

## BAT CABLE

This special cable is used in most of Batman's tools, developed privately in WayneTech's industrial department. Like the Bat Cuffs, only a diamond-edged cutting instrument can slice through this cable. The Bat Cable in the Bat Cuffs is used to restrain criminals, while the Bat Cable in the Bat Grapple enables Batman to rise to or descend from city rooftops.

When the Bat Cable is selected on the utility belt, Batman attaches a Batarang to the end of the cable, hooks it onto an overhead corner or pipe, and swings forward in the direction in which he's facing. As the momentum carries Batman forward, press the Jump button or the Use button to dismount. Using the Jump button is a little wiser, since you can press it again at the height of your jump off the cable to perform a flip, thus going even further.

The more times Batman swings back and forth, the less momentum each swing will have. As long as Batman is still moving, you can increase the arc of the swing.

When using the Bat Cable, Batman immediately swings forward in the direction in which he's facing. Also, it's highly recommended that you first use an item in First-Person View to line up the intended trajectory. The Batarang is on the utility belt just a notch below the Bat Cable, so aim the Batarang using First-Person View to line up the correct position before switching back to the Bat Cable and swinging across.

## SMOKE CAPSULE

Batman carries a small supply of capsules that break on impact and release a cloud of diluted nerve gas that obscures vision or knocks out a person temporarily. The effect varies depending on how well the Smoke Capsule is targeted. If a foe gets hit directly in the head with the capsule, it will knock the foe unconscious for a time. To obscure someone's vision, throw the capsule at the person's torso or make it land directly in front of the foe.

Use Smoke Capsules to get past large enemy groups. After tossing a Smoke Capsule at a group of thugs, they will attempt to wave the smoke from their eyes. When this occurs, run past them or knock out the enemies if needed.

## MEDICAL KIT

The Medical Kit enables Batman to cure toxins and viral agents. It also helps to rejuvenate wounded tissue and recover from wounds. Medical Kits come in two sizes, dependent on the deployment of equipment selected during the last "Game Over" and continuation. A Small Medical Kit replenishes up to 200 health points, while a Large Medical Kit refills up to 400.

If the Medical Kit is selected on the utility belt, and it has some rejuvenation points left, then it will be used automatically if Batman's health points get reduced to zero. Therefore, it's a good idea to equip the Medical Kit when Batman is forced to square off against tough archenemies, such as Killer Croc and The Joker.

# ITEMS

There are many different items in the game, most of which add to the underlying story and explain some of the more subtle elements of the plot. Some of the items also help to explain what needs to be done to complete a certain task in the game, while other items are needed to progress past certain obstacles. Here's a list of the items in *Batman: Dark Tomorrow*.

## GOTHAM GAZETTE–LATE CITY EDITION

### GANG WAR IMMINENT IN GOTHAM!

Late last night, a group of individuals wearing elaborate Halloween masks made a raid on Gotham First National Bank, stealing approximately $500,000 in cash. The men, who are believed to be a part of the False Face Society—a criminal gang run by Roman Sionis, aka Black Mask—are currently being sought by the GCPD. They are considered extremely dangerous and must not be approached.

Sources at the GCPD indicate that this robbery was likely committed to fund Black Mask's plan to take control of the crime syndicate in Gotham, which is currently run by Arnold Wesker, aka The Ventriloquist. Wesker, who was recently paroled from Arkham Asylum, suffers from multiple personality disorder, which has in the past produced Scarface, the crime boss personality who runs the syndicate. The Ventriloquist and Scarface are believed to have ties to many Gotham businesses, particularly Gotham City Shipping, which is located and run out of Dixon Docks. The GCPD has issued the following statement…

## NEWSTIME MAGAZINE

### EXCLUSIVE

### Police Commissioner James Gordon—The Interview

When I sat down to interview Gotham City Police Commissioner James Gordon, I found him to be the epitome of the tough no-nonsense cop—a reputation that has surrounded him since his early days in the Chicago Police Department. In fact, it was Gordon who asked that we skip all of my preliminary questions and cut right to the chase. So I immediately asked him about the crime that so obviously runs rampant on the streets of Gotham. According to Gordon: "Gotham, like every other city in the world, has its share of crime. The difference is that our criminals tend to be a little more… extreme than your average mugger. However, the police are working hard to protect the citizens of Gotham, to keep the streets safe, and to reduce the overall crime rate."

## WORK RELEASE FORM (IN TALBOT FACTORY)

This item indicates that ventilation crews have cleared out the main air duct in the Talbot factory, allowing for increased ventilation, and also access for Batman to enter the Underground Sewers.

## INSIDE GOTHAM MAGAZINE

### INVESTIGATION
### The Revolving Door of Arkham Asylum
~Part Two~

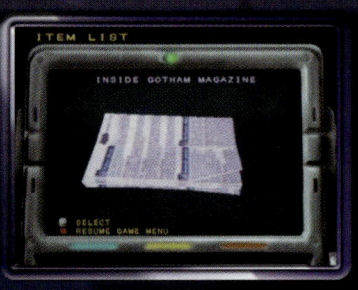

In Part Two of our expose on **Arkham Asylum**, we continue our exclusive, undercover interview with one of the asylum's own employees to learn if the home for the criminally insane is actually helping—or hurting—the inmates who reside in its hallowed halls. For safety reasons, the employee will again be known only as "Smith."

**IG:** *Okay, let's turn our attention to the inmates. Arkham certainly has its share of celebrities. They're so popular, in fact, that most of them are not even known by their real names, but by media-dubbed criminal nicknames: Poison Ivy, Mr. Freeze, Killer Croc. This list goes on. But is there one particular inmate you would consider to be the most dangerous, or the most insane?*

**Smith:** Yeah, that's an easy one, The Joker. They don't get worse. He... I don't know, he just gets inside your head and messes you up!

## MEMORANDUM (IN ASYLUM)

### ARKHAM ASYLUM
### MEMO

**From:** Michael Beacham, Chief Engineer
**To:** Jeremiah Arkham, Director
**Re:** Water Temperature in Waylon Jones' Cell

Just wanted to inform you that work has been completed on the control valves that regulate the water temperature in Killer Croc's cell. The temperature has been raised 10 degrees to increase Croc's body temperature and keep him more comfortable. It should be known that if Croc becomes a problem, then decreasing the water temperature in the boiler room will slow him down substantially.

## COMPUTER EMAIL

**From:** Johnson@Arkham.asylum
**Re:** Current Inmate Activity

Jeremiah.

Regarding your recent inquiry into the inmates' morale and activities, the observations from my security teams, as well as my own personal opinion, have lead to the following conclusion: Through fear and intimidation "The Joker" is slowly amassing a larger following of inmates than originally expected. The numbers now total in the upper 30s, with the inmates spread throughout the entire asylum. The more disturbed inmates, from the maximum-security wing, have even taken to "decorating" their straightjackets so that no one will mistake them for being anything other than "The Joker's Men." Needless to say, the less problematic patients are now living in fear. They don't want to submit to The Joker's rule, but are afraid for their lives if they reject his offer. Obviously, this is not the first time that such factions controlled by "The Joker" or any other inmate (such as Harvey Dent or Jonathan Crane) have arisen inside Arkham. The key to controlling this problem will be detailed in my weekly report, although it is clear that an increase in well-trained security guards, as well as more experienced doctors and nurses, would certainly be the biggest help. Feel free to contact me if you have any questions.

Robert

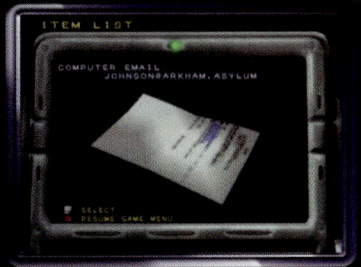

## COMPUTER EMAIL

**From:** Booden@Arkham.asylum
**Re:** Hey...

Hey Deb.

Yeah, I was there yesterday when the cops brought in Nigma. And yes, Laura was there too, and I think it finally completed her picture of Jeremiah. Of course, Nigma had to mention Batman (which I think he does just to get a rise out of Arkham) and Jeremiah went ballistic. Laura wasn't close enough to really hear the whole thing, but it was good. Later, she came up to me and asked about Jeremiah, and why he overreacted when Eddie's riddle indirectly mentioned Batman. I told her flat-out that Jeremiah believes that half of the crazies who are in here wouldn't be here if there wasn't a Batman, and that he thinks that Bats is just as nutty as the rest of 'em. We just have to toughen her up a bit, but I think she'll do fine. Ol' Jervis has been complaining about everything lately. I told him before that he was mad—lol! Talk to you later...

Val

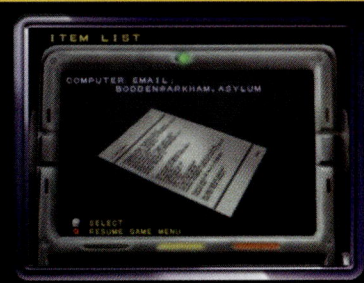

## COMPUTER EMAIL

**From:** Address Unkown
**Re:** Commander Helson

Long live the Demon's Head. The mission in Gotham City was a success. Team Alpha received the shipment, met with representatives from both sides, and supplied them with the necessary equipment. Team Beta handled the matter at police headquarters. Team Gamma made all of the necessary arrangements at Arkham Asylum. All three teams have regrouped at Checkpoint Seven-B, and are currently en route to Bunker Zero-Zero-One in the safe zone. Next report will be in six hours.

Cpt. T. Bava

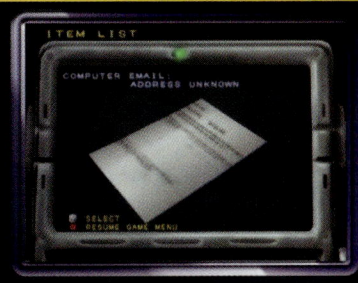

## COMPUTER EMAIL

**From:** Address Unkown
**Re:** Zeta Team

Commander Smythe

Transmission received from Zeta team. At the Master's request, they have made the final checks of the detonators and incendiary devices located in section Six-Five. All is ready and awaiting the Master's command. Zeta team has been repositioned at Station Three-A and will remain there until otherwise notified. Long live the Demon's Head.

Cpt. H. Miller

# UTILITY BELT

## PERSONAL NOTES

Re: Demon's Head

I have finally encountered Talia, the daughter of the Demon's Head himself. She is, as all rumors suggest, exquisite, and that makes the prospect of working for her father and for her all the more dangerous—and profitable. While her physical presence is striking, her confidence and command over the men is that of a seasoned veteran. And despite all of the Master's previous plans, she seems particularly interested in this one—specifically, in our operations surrounding Gotham City. Regarding Gotham, it should be noted that reports have her linked romantically to Batman. While there may be a small modicum of truth in those reports, I cannot believe them entirely, for I am certain that there is no man who would be able to resist her.

## PERSONAL NOTES

Re: Demon's Head

The time is near. All teams have reported in, and the operation is proceeding according to plan. All systems are operational, and are awaiting the final survey and eventual command, of the Demon's Head. The Master's plan will soon be realized and all will be as it once was. Through death, there will be life. There will be a new Eden, and I will be there to see it.

## DEFOLIANT
Pick up this item just before the showdown with Poison Ivy.

## HIGH-ACCESS SECURITY CLEARANCE CARD
Obtain this from Arkham after saving him from Mr. Freeze in the upper levels of the Arkham Asylum.

## ARKHAM ASYLUM PASS KEY
Take from Dr. McKee, who is trapped in Killer Croc's cell. After defeating Killer Croc, get the key to his cell off of his body. Then open the door and get the Pass Key from the doctor.

# AMMUNITION CRATES 1, 2, 3

**Crate 1**: Modified Infantry Anti-Tank Weapon. Original model used in WWII. Caution: Estimated increase in range and firepower by 115% due to recent modifications.

**Additional Information:** Found in Warehouse District.

**Crate 2**: Modified Infantry Anti-Tank Weapon. Original model used in WWII. Caution: Estimated increase in range and firepower by 115% due to recent modifications.

**Additional Information:** Found in Warehouse District.

**Crate 3**: Modified Infantry Anti-Tank Weapon. Original model used in WWII. Caution: Estimated increase in range and firepower by 115% due to recent modifications.

**Additional Information:** Found in Rā's al Ghūl's Castle.

# GAME BASICS

This chapter attempts to acquaint you with the basic control of *Batman: Dark Tomorrow*, and teach you how to outwit the half-wits working for the crime bosses of Gotham.

## GAME MENU FUNCTIONS

Press the Menu button at any time during the game to access the Game Menu. The various options here enable you to view the Batgear items up close, as well as other items of evidence gathered from crime scenes. Batman also carries a complete database of allies and villains.

The Game Options sub-menu enables you to tweak some of the game's settings to better suit your style of playing. The Brightness setting in the game is somewhat low, essentially for mood and ambience. To see the on-screen environment better, use a brighter setting.

Some of the on-screen displays can become more transparent (for example, the Status Display in the bottom-left corner of the screen, as well as the Bat Radar display in the top-right corner of the screen). Probably the most important function in the Game Options sub-menu is the ability to adjust the range of the radar. By default, the setting is 100 ft. Much wider settings, such as 150ft and 200ft, will display more of the map. When using these options, the downside is that it becomes nearly impossible to spot enemies. For those looking for stealth-like gameplay, the recommended setting is 50ft. This should enable you to pinpoint the enemies on the radar more precisely.

The Game Menu also provides the method by which you can save your game. You can save your game at any time, provided that a memory device is inserted into the console. When loading a saved game, the adventure resumes at the start of the level. It should be noted that any enemies that have been properly restrained are removed from the level.

## BAT RADAR

Probably the most important and useful tool is the Bat Radar, which is displayed in the upper-right corner of the screen. The Bat Radar automatically detects the layout of the environment. A white arrow indicates Batman's position, and points in the direction in which Batman is currently facing. Enemy positions within a 50-foot radius are marked on the map, and their field of vision is also illustrated in a cone shape. The colors of an enemy's markers and cone of vision changes depending on the situation.

- **White Dot:** Civilian.
- **Green Dot:** Location of an enemy who has *not* detected Batman.
- **Red Dot:** Enemy who has detected Batman and is attacking.
- **Orange Dot:** Enemy who has been knocked down, but will get back up again soon.
- **Yellow Dot:** Enemy who has been properly restrained and is no longer active.
- **Green Cone:** Enemy has *not* spotted Batman.
- **Dark Green Cone:** A noise has alerted the enemy. This means that the enemy is watching, but has *not* spotted Batman.
- **Red Cone:** The enemy has spotted Batman or knows his location and is moving to attack.

### BAT RADAR: BETTER THAN THE HUMAN EYE?
The game's camera tends to be a little tight around Batman at all times. Rely on tools such as the Bat Radar and Corner Peeking (described later in this chapter) to maintain Batman's cover. Use these tools to your advantage to plot a successful strategy for infiltration.

## BASICS OF MOVEMENT

In this stealth-based action game, character control is the first step to success. There are various "modes" of movement, and you can easily toggle between them.

- **Standing:** The default movement mode is "Standing." As camera angles change, Batman will continue running in the same direction. There is no need to move him to compensate for changes in the view. Once he stops moving, the directions will reset for the new camera angle. Batman can even walk very quickly but quietly. The advantage of standing movement is that Batman can cross a large area very quickly. The downside is that enemies are more likely to see or hear him moving, especially if he's running.

- **Sneaking:** While standing upright, press the Mode button once to make Batman hunch over. This is called "Sneak" mode. While in this mode, Batman can only move at a very slow speed but he does so silently. Use Sneak mode whenever enemies appear on the Bat Radar to avoid being heard. While in Sneak mode, it's possible for Batman to creep up behind an enemy and apply the Sleeper Hold. Sneaking is the safe way to go when enemies aren't aware of Batman's location.

- **Crouching:** While in Sneak mode, press the Mode button a second time to "crouch." While crouched low to the ground, Batman moves slowly. He can hide behind objects and obstacles in the environment, and enemies are less likely to spot him. While in a crouching position, press the Jump button to roll forward silently. Use the forward roll to avoid enemy fistfights or bullets. Batman can't use the Medicine Kit while crouching.

### WARNING
Silent ingress into criminal territory is Batman's best means of outwitting his opponents. If a villain spots Batman or hears him, the criminal will signal to his comrades. Batman's fists are useless against a large group of thugs, so the ability to "sneak" through most of the game and act with caution is important to master.

## ROLLING: THE FASTEST SNEAKING METHOD

As mentioned earlier, enemies are more likely to hear Batman's movements when he charges into an area like a freight train. Therefore, it's important to spend a majority of the game in sneak mode. However, movement in sneak mode can be rather slow. To speed things up, sneak across areas quickly and quietly by repeatedly crouching and rolling.

For example, let's say Batman is attempting to sneak up on an enemy to take him down, but the enemy tends to turn around every few seconds. Use the forward roll to come up behind this cautious thug in a split second. Then quickly knock him out and Batcuff him before he calls for help. While hiding behind some crates and an enemy walks by on patrol, sneak up behind him quickly and take him down before he turns around.

## WALL MOVEMENT AND CORNER VIEW

When close to a flat wall, press the Wall Sneak button to make Batman flatten himself against it. While up against the wall, press left or right to make Batman move quietly along the wall. Use this technique to enter very narrow areas.

When Batman reaches a corner of a wall, press the move button again to make him lean out. The view then shifts to First-Person Perspective. Now Batman can see around the corner with little chance of being spotted. While in this corner view, select and use attack items such as Batarangs and Smoke Capsules. This is possibly the best way to get the jump on enemies, so approach each corner with the wall press/corner view technique in mind!

## ENEMY RESTRAINT

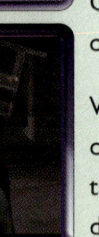

When dealing with criminals of all types, the objective is to take them by surprise, knock them to the ground, and restrain them with Batcuffs before they regain consciousness and alert others. The best method to use to apply Batcuffs is with the Quick Restraint button.

Not all crooks remain unconscious for the same amount of time. When Batman knocks out a foe with his bare hands, the enemy will hop back on his feet shortly. When using the Batarangs or Smoke Capsules, the enemy will remain prone for a much longer period of time. Unfortunately, Batman can only carry a limited supply of these attack items.

When fighting groups of enemies, all stealth tactics fly out the window and survival becomes a matter of martial arts prowess. Before attempting to apply the Batcuffs to an individual in a group, make sure that *absolutely everyone* is knocked out and then use restraints on only two or more individuals. After doing so, additional enemies will regain consciousness, so be prepared to knock them down again.

## SWINGING AND JUMPING

The first skill you need to master is the art of swinging from rooftop to rooftop using the Bat Cable. To swing, select the Bat Cable from the Utility Belt menu in the lower-left corner of the screen and press the Use button. This makes Batman immediately start swinging in the direction in which he's facing. Press the Jump or Use buttons to release the Bat Cable when you reach another platform. Positioning Batman correctly before starting to swing is the key to a successful swing.

The easiest way to line up a swing is to equip an item that uses First-Person View (such as Nightvision, the Batarang or the Smoke Capsule). Stand at the edge of the area from which you want to swing, equip the Batarang, and rotate the view so that it points directly at the target landing area. Then press the Jump button to cancel the use of the Batarang, press left on the D-pad once to equip the Batcable, and press the Use button to start swinging. Using First-Person View before launching almost always ensures a precise swing.

If the distance to swing is greater than the arc that the length of the Bat Cable allows, then climb up to higher levels. The same tip holds true if the target landing area is on a slightly higher level than the launching platform. Also, hold the directional button in the direction that Batman is traveling for a more powerful swing. Therefore, when the Bat Cable is released, the forward momentum should safely carry Batman to the landing area.

If Batman still falls a little short of the intended landing area, then double-tap the Jump button upon dismount to execute a flip. This increases Batman's forward momentum, hopefully carrying him onto the intended landing area. Swinging will take some practice, and it's the one of the first things you need to master in the game.

### KNOW YOUR UTILITIES
Remember that the Bat Cable is used as a tool for swinging forward, while the Bat Grapple is utilized to ascend or descend to different levels.

## BATARANG TARGETING

Batarangs are used to knock out enemies quietly from a distance. They can be selected and used while in Sneak, Crouch or Corner View modes. When selected in the Utility Belt window, press the Use button to enter First-Person targeting mode. Adjust the view until the crosshairs lock onto a criminal, then press the Punch button to throw a Batarang. If the target is moving, the throw could miss even if the crosshairs are locked on to the target.

A single Batarang can disable single *or* multiple opponents. For example, if a group of hoods is positioned in front of exploding barrels, aim for a barrel instead of one of the hoods. The blast will knock out all the enemies within the blast radius. If there are other barrels in the same area, they will also explode in a chain reaction that will render most of the enemies in an area unconscious!

Sometimes, using a Batarang to take down one enemy causes him to yell out or make noise as he drops. This reaction could draw the attention of other villains in the area, causing them to investigate their fallen comrade. If someone comes to the aid of the downed foe, use another Batarang on the new arrival. If this draws the attention of others, then you might soon collect a whole bunch of unconscious bad guys with very little effort!

Once thrown, Batarangs remain visible on the ground for a short period of time, or until you throw another one. Retrieve Batarangs on the ground and use them again! Simply move over them to return the device to your inventory.

## WAYNETECH BOXES

Expert players who have little trouble moving through the criminal-infested neighborhoods could run into one small dilemma: running out of equipment! Fortunately, there are WAYNETECH boxes in various locations throughout the city. Use them to restock offensive items, as well as medical supplies.

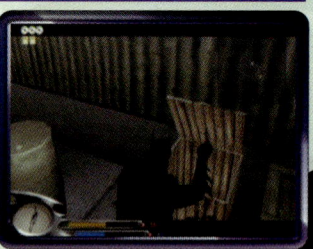

Most WAYNETECH boxes are found indoors inside "secret" or locked rooms. Use the contents of the boxes to restock supplies as many times as needed in any of the three deployment modes listed in the "Utility Belt" chapter. If Batman is low on health and armor when reaching a WAYNETECH box, use a Medical Kit before loading up. This way, the WAYNETECH box is left with a full complement of armaments and first aid.

## MOBILITY AND ATTACK WITH NIGHTVISION

When using the Nightvision goggles, the game switches to First-Person View. All light in the area is focused through an electronic spectrum, illuminating surfaces and people who might otherwise remain hidden in normal view. As a result, the Nightvision goggles also reveal hidden laser trip mines, which might set off booby traps if triggered.

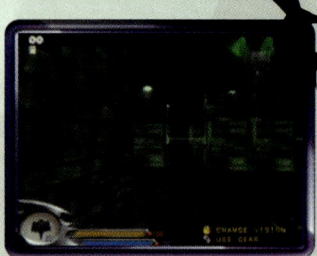

Batman can still move, crouch and perform melee attacks when using the Nightvision goggles. Also, Batman can use all of his equipment (such as Batarangs and Smoke Capsules) while Nightvision is engaged, and the Medical Kit if he's standing. If another item is selected on the Utility Belt, you must scroll through the items back to the Nightvision icon to disengage the goggles.

> **NAVIGATING LASER TRIP MINES**
> When using Nightvision, Batman can roll under laser beams. To do so, move up to the beam, crouch, and press the Roll button. When successful, Batman should travel right under the beam.

## SLEEPER HOLD

By sneaking up behind a stationary opponent, take down the foe in style by pressing the Punch button. The effect of the Sleeper Hold doesn't last as long as a sharp blow from a Batarang, but the close proximity to the thug allows for swift use of the Batcuffs!

## JUDO CHOP

Another option for a sneak attack from the rear is the classic Judo Chop. Creep up behind a foe, press the Mode button, then press the Use button. This makes Batman deliver one quick chop to the target's neck, rendering him instantly unconscious. This move is just as effective as the Sleeper Hold.

# MELEE COMBAT

When stealth fails and detection has occurred, it's time to resort to martial arts. The two basic methods of melee combat include punches and kicks. The strength of these physical attacks can vary depending on the position and distance of the target. The level of the attack is registered both in the power of the force feedback felt in the controller, as well as the color of the burst particle displayed on-screen. Here's a breakdown:

 White = Low power     Yellow = Medium power     Red = Knockout blows

Red hits are usually achieved through the proper timing of movement and attacking. For this reason, melee combat is most effective when Batman is standing upright.

- **Punch:** Press the Punch button to perform a punch. Tap the Punch button rapidly to execute an alternating combination of blows. Batman can also punch when in Sneak and Crouch modes.
- **Kick:** Press the Kick button to perform a kick. The default kick is a head-level attack. Move toward the enemy and press Kick simultaneously to perform a low kick, which may have the effect of "tripping" a walking target.
- **Roundhouse Kick:** When standing stationary in front of an enemy, hold down on the control pad a brief moment before pressing the Kick button to execute a powerful Roundhouse. This move almost always results in a knockout.
- **Haymaker:** While running toward an opponent at full speed, press the Punch button with the proper timing. This unleashes a powerful thrust jab, which almost always results in a knockout.
- **Superkick:** While running toward an enemy at full speed, press the Kick button with the proper timing to perform a pivot kick. This move almost always results in a red hit knockout.
- **Leg Sweep:** While crouching, press the Kick button to make Batman sweep the ground with his leg, tripping all opponents within range. Because of the damage inflicted when an enemy falls, this move almost always results in a knockout. If Batman gets knocked to the ground, he will perform a Leg Sweep while rising if the Kick button is pressed with the right timing.
- **Jump Kick:** Use the Jump Kick when surrounded on all sides by enemies. Press the Jump button followed immediately by the Kick or Punch button with the proper timing. This makes Batman spin in midair and kick all opponents (those at close range) in the face. Enemies at extremely close range may suffer a knockout.

# GAME OVER AND CONTINUES

As you begin this dark crusade for justice, you'll need time to develop the skills required to defeat lots of enemies. When Batman's health runs out, the Game Over screen appears. Select the "Continue" option to restart the game in the last area. You'll have an opportunity to restock all of your Batgear before plunging in again.

The game continues from the entrance of the room in which Batman lost all of his health, with all of the enemies reset to their default states. Be warned that the thugs patrolling the area might already be alerted to your presence. Reassess the situation before proceeding.

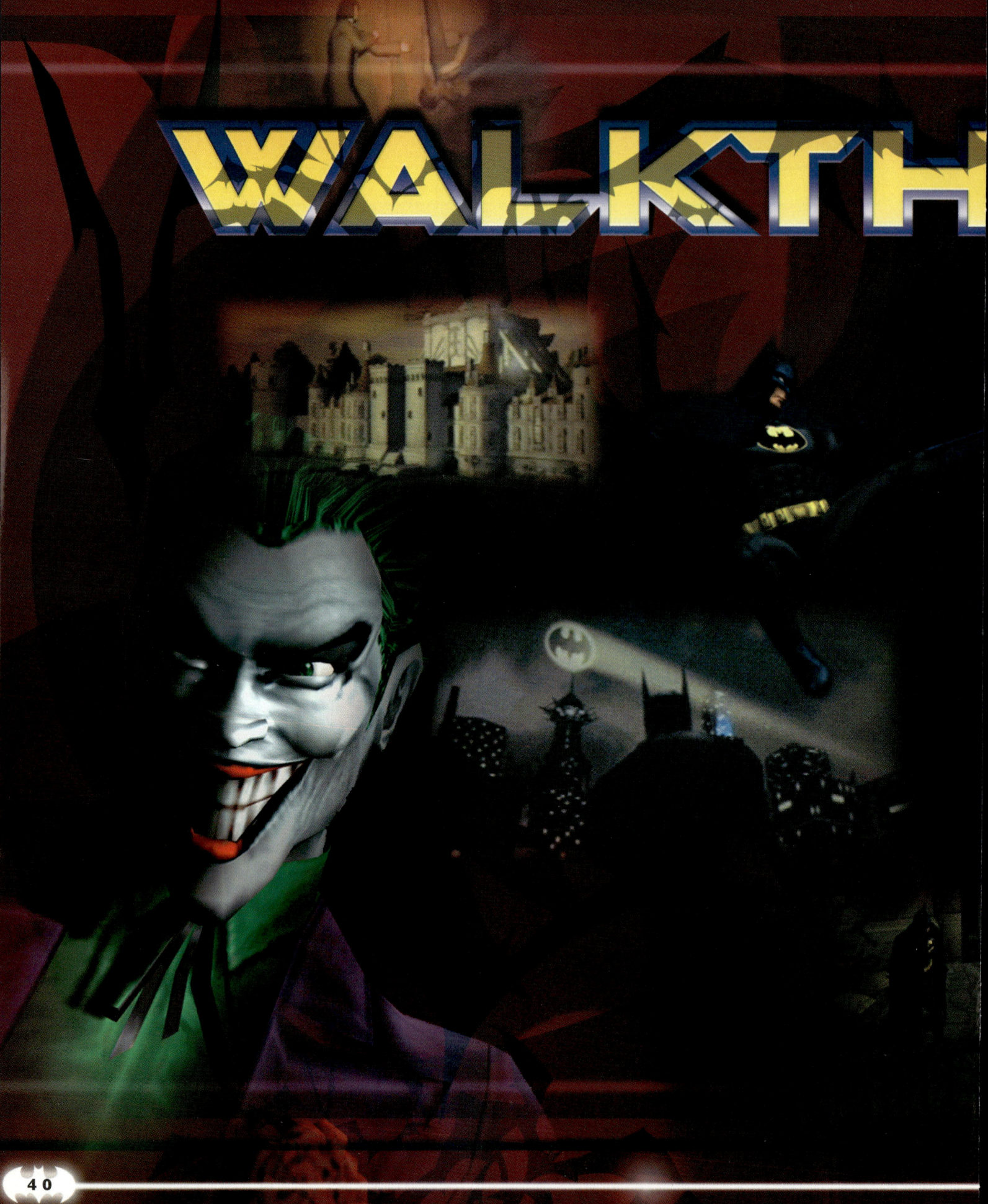

ROUGH

# PRELUDE

While *Batman: Dark Tomorrow* is largely a linear game, sneaking through the lairs of criminals can be accomplished in more than one way. For example, some areas contain Music CDs or Sketchbooks that you don't necessarily have to find to defeat the game. This section of the guide attempts to describe the easiest and safest method by which to cross each area while still ensuring that all secrets are unlocked.

# PRELUDE

The first two areas of this game (Robbery in Progress and the Gotham Rooftops) provide an opportunity to become more accustomed to the controls necessary for fighting, running, and jumping. It's also a great time to become acquainted with the cool accessories in the game. After making it across the rooftop to the Commissioner, the real fun begins!

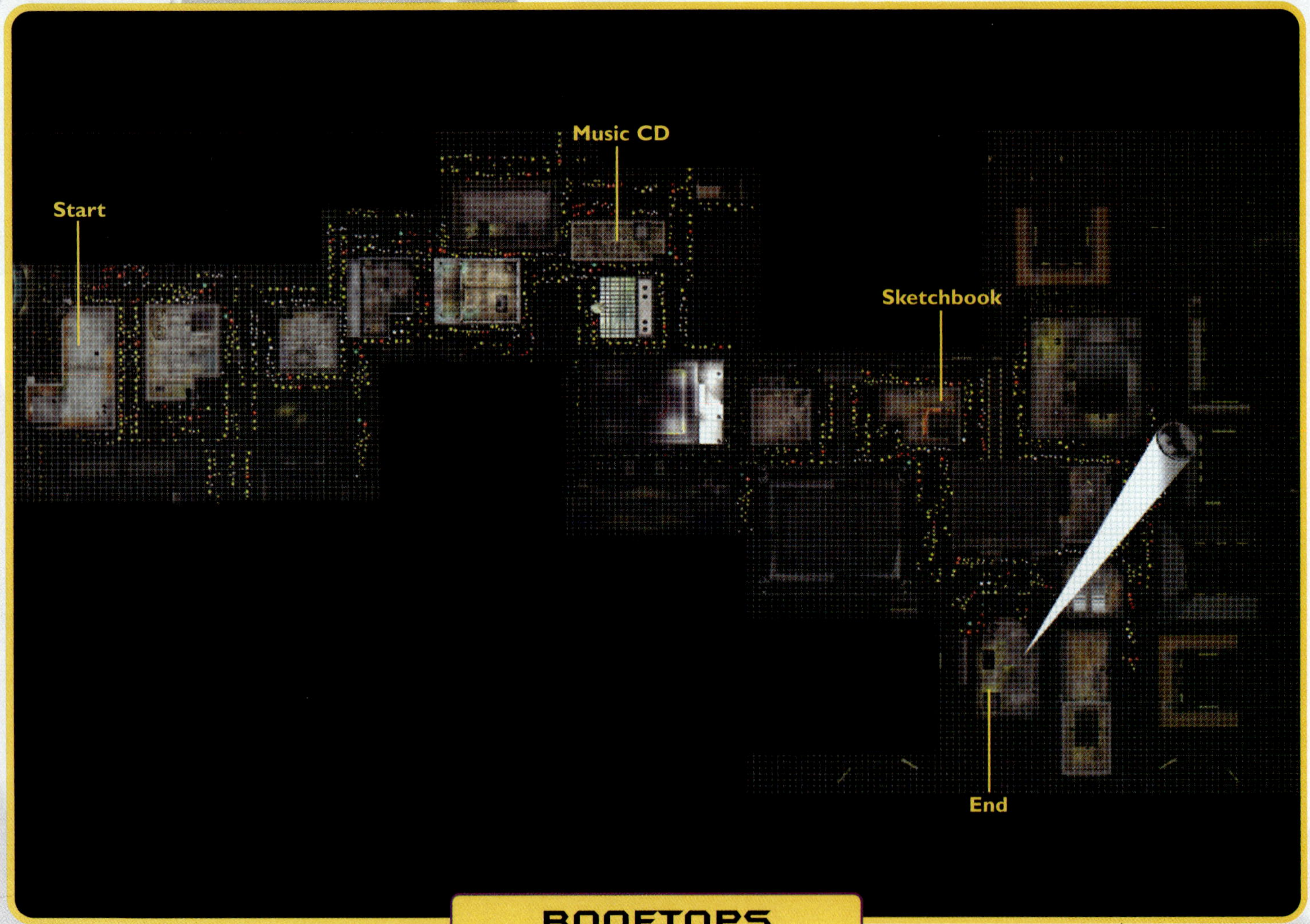

## ROOFTOPS

## ROBBERY IN PROGRESS!

As the game begins, Batman drops into an alleyway and fights some common thugs. Since they are armed only with knives or their bare knuckles, take this opportunity to learn the game's basic melee combat controls. Try punching, kicking, and jump-kicking to disable all three. After knocking down all of the crooks, place a set of Batcuffs on them and watch the rest of the cut-scene.

*Applying the Batcuffs will ensure that the enemies stay down.*

**WARNING**

After getting knocked to the ground, the crooks won't stay there for long. They will eventually come to their senses and attack again. For this reason, it's important to have the Batcuffs ready to bind their hands and keep them down for good.

*There will be a call to the rooftops with the Bat Signal.*

## BATMAN & AERODYNAMICS

Once on the rooftops, it's time for a little Batcable-swinging action. Learning how to swing from rooftop to rooftop is a challenge at first, but your skills will improve substantially in a very short time. While crossing this dangerous area, you may plummet to the ground once or twice. Swing in the wrong direction or dismount too soon, and you may not make it to the other side.

*Swinging over toward the left edge of the building results in a nasty fall.*

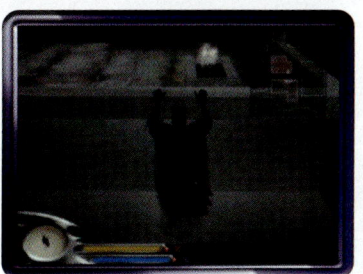

*If the jump is off by a little, Batman may still grab the ledge and pull himself up!*

When using the Bat Cable to swing across an area, it's important to ensure that Batman is facing the exact location to which you want to swing. To make sure everything is properly lined up, equip the Batarang and look around in First-Person View. When the intended landing zone is within view, switch to the Batcable and swing across.

## SWINGING PAST OBSTACLES AND HAZARDS

Use Batman's Batcable to cross the first two rooftops with ease. Just run to the edge, get properly aligned with the next rooftop, then use the Batcable. The fourth rooftop is much higher than the third one, so move to the right and climb the ladder to the top of the water tank. Utilize the First-Person View of the Batarang, and position Batman so that he's looking at the small building on the fourth roof. This should ensure a safe swing across this wide gap.

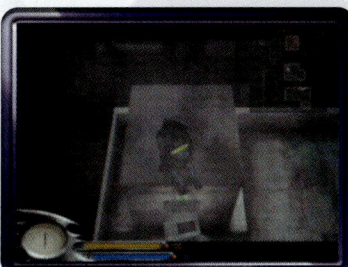

*Climbing up to the highest point will provide an advantage when swinging across large gaps.*

*Use the Batarang's First-Person View to line up Batman's intended destination.*

*Use the same technique for the next Bat Cable jump. Get to the highest point, line it up, then do it!*

# PRELUDE

## CLIMBING ONTO LEDGES & PROPER JUMPING TECHNIQUE

The next rooftop is close enough that you don't need to swing across it, but there is a danger of falling if the jump isn't performed correctly. Run against the ledge of the rooftop and press the Jump button. Batman should safely climb onto the thin ledge. Move forward and simultaneously press the Jump button again to easily clear the gap.

*This jump requires solid timing with the Jump button.*

*Three more jumps to get to the helicopter pad, which is visible in the upper-left corner of this screenshot.*

Make an angled swing to the next rooftop, then move toward the ledge on the right and use the method previously mentioned to make Batman stand on the ledge. The following ledge will also be a jump down. Approach the ledge and press the Jump button when close to it to get into perfect jumping position. After doing so, jump to the slanted rooftop made of glass. A running jump will accomplish this task. From this location, jump to the helicopter pad.

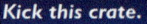

There is a **Music CD** hidden inside the crate on the rooftop near the helicopter pad. Kick the crate to open it and find the Music CD. One good kick should do the trick!

*Kick this crate.*

*Voila! Your first goodie!*

## THE LAST SERIES OF ROOFTOPS

Now that you understand the complexities of the Bat Cable, swing from the middle of the helicopter pad across the next two rooftops.

There is a **Sketchbook** hidden inside the barrels on the rooftop before the crosswalk. Use Batman's Batarang to blow them up and expose the book.

*Blow up these barrels.*

*The first Sketchbook is just waiting to be picked up.*

## THE RAVAGES OF GANG WAR

While the gangs wage war, many innocent civilians get caught in the crossfire. Batman enters the fray just as three creeps begin chasing some helpless person into a dark alley. Quickly run at each thug and perform a hard attack to knock them each out with one blow. When all three are on the ground, restrain each crook with the Batcuffs. If not, they'll be back on their feet again!

Let the civilians run past before unleashing against the thugs.

There is a dead end down the first turn to the left. It may look like nothing but bad news, but take the route anyway to find another **Music CD**.

The Music CD is at the back of this dead-end alley.

The rocket is en route in this screenshot. Stay next to the building to remain safely out of reach.

## ROCKET LAUNCHER

Move down the alleyway to the corner, and use Batman's Bat Radar to spot an enemy. This thug, armed with a rocket launcher, is waiting on the second floor of the building. Also, his attack area is displayed as a green cone. To avoid being hit by the rocket launcher, stay close to the building and sneak underneath the enemy's window. Note that once the crook fires one rocket and misses, he won't fire again.

Double-jump onto the hood of the wrecked truck, then jump and grab the windowsill below the thug. After doing so, jump into the room to find two enemies. After a short cut-scene, attack the guy with the rocket launcher. After disposing of him, the second thug runs out of the room.

### SEARCH THE AREA
Don't rush out of the room just yet. Before leaving, pick up a copy of the **Gotham Gazette**!

# GOTHAM CITY ALLEYWAY

Leave the room through the door and enter the hallway. There are several doors here that you can try to open, but even with the use of Batman's Universal Tool, only one of them will open. Find the unlocked door and proceed into the alleyway behind the building.

## DANGEROUS ALLEYS

While in the alleyway, Batman spots the "one that got away." Don't worry; it's okay to let him go. Hop down off the walkway into the alley. Locate the car parked on the left side of the alleyway. Move past this car too quickly, and the resulting explosion will cause a lot of damage. Instead, enter Stealth Mode and sneak past the car. Stay as far away from the car as possible.

*Batman must sneak past this car or it will explode!*

Once past the car, it's imperative that you follow the route indicated on the map. If not, you'll get gunned down in a flurry of bullets and explosives. Near the end of the first alleyway, take a right through the narrow passage. If you reject this advice, you'll get shot down before you can take five steps to the left.

The goal is to follow the "guy that got away." Move through the outdoor café area, then around to the next street. Although you can see the green attack cone of the enemy, he always moves away when you approach, so just keep moving.

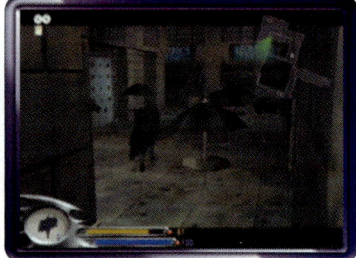

*The streets remain deserted, so continue to follow the hoodlum.*

### JUST A REMINDER...
Although there are lots of doors in the alleys and streets, none of them are unlocked. Also, there are no Music CDs or Sketchbooks to find in this area.

Upon reaching the burning truck, stick to the right side of the street and slowly approach the flaming mess. Batman can pass through the narrow area on the right. As noted earlier, the other path is full of gunfire. Proceed past the fire to move into the next area, Gazette Square.

# GAZETTE SQUARE

This is the center of the action! Black Mask and his gang are actively facing off against a horde of Scarface followers in and around Gazette Square. There are plenty of civilians, so take measures to avoid any unnecessary casualties. Something *must* be done to contain these hooligans before they destroy Gotham City!

This city belongs to me.

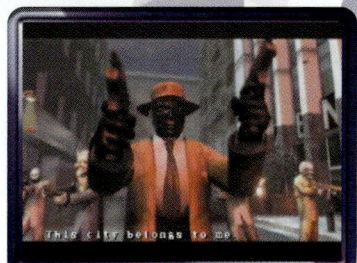

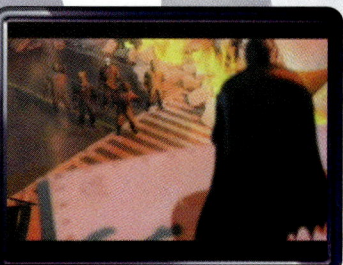

*Time for Batman to properly take care of the situation!*

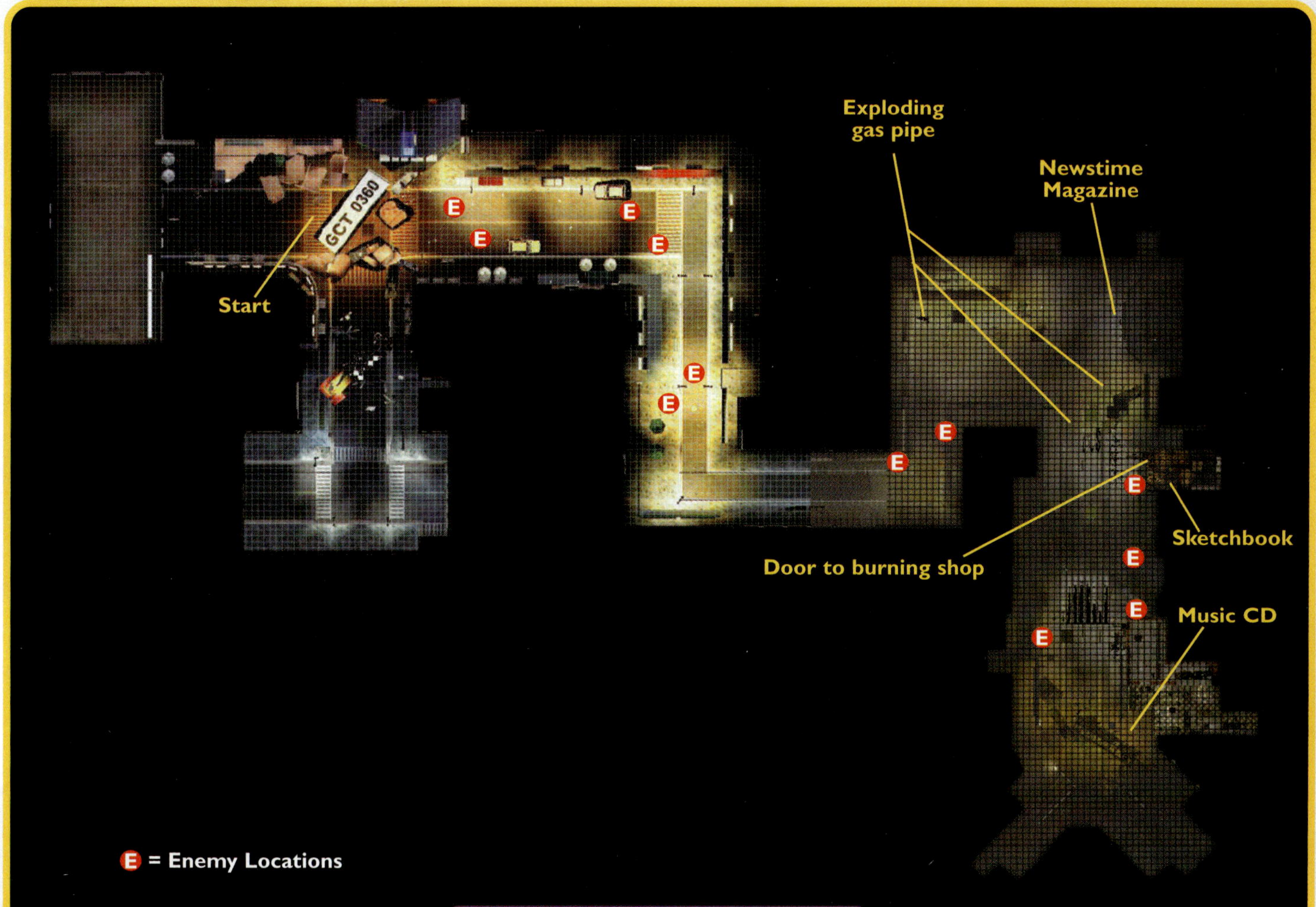
Exploding gas pipe
Newstime Magazine
GCT 0360
Start
Sketchbook
Door to burning shop
Music CD
E = Enemy Locations

GAZETTE SQUARE

# GAZETTE SQUARE

## ACTION!

The action begins immediately with several of Black Mask's crew approaching with guns blazing. To eliminate this threat, run at them (weave or jump to avoid the gunfire), then execute a power attack to put them down one at a time. Remember that they will get up after a few moments, so knock them out and secure them with Batman's Batcuffs.

*Run for the enemy. You may take a hit or two, but it's the best way to take them down quickly.*

After subduing the first wave of attackers, slowly move to the north. As Batman approaches the red car, two more thugs appear. They will *both* use their guns, but a jump-kick and a few blows to the head will dispose of them. Use Batman's Batcuffs on these goons, then move to the corner that turns to the right. Go into Stealth Mode so that the two Black Mask cronies are oblivious to their surroundings. Then use s Batarang and let them have it! If the cronies spot Batman, prepare for another fight.

*The Batarang can take down enemies even at close range.*

## THE DARK AND LONELY ALLEY

After cuffing the rest of the bad guys, move down the street and hang a left into a darkened alley with a wrecked car in it. Several civilians will run around the corner, but don't ignore them—they're being chased and their pursuers aren't far behind! Move past the car and sneak up to the corner at the end of alley, then wait for one of Black Mask's crew to show his face.

*Make sure both bad guys are down before using the Batcuffs.*

Just around the corner are two or three more gang members, all armed with tommy guns. Dispose of them as quickly as possible, then subdue them before they can get up and cause more damage. At this point, it's best to equip a Medical Kit to replenish any lost health before moving on.

## THE STREET OF PAIN

The next area is punctuated by burning businesses on either side of the street with debris littered everywhere. Be very careful while moving down this area, because the fire will rob Batman of valuable health units in he comes in contact with it. Also, be aware of the open areas in the middle of the street. Passing too close to them will cause severe damage!

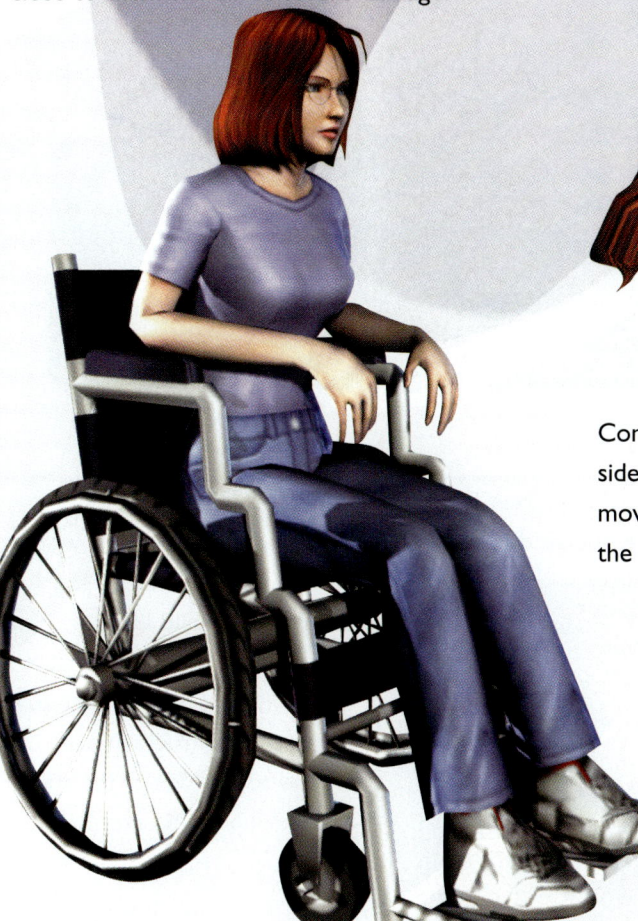

### WARNING
Be wary of any exposed gas pipes in the middle of the street. If Batman gets too close, he will suffer massive amounts of damage from fire or explosions.

Continue down the street and move toward the deserted area on the right side to find a copy of **Newstime Magazine**. After picking it up, continue to move down the street.

*Grab the copy of Newstime Magazine; it may help clear up some of the mystery.*

## THE CROOKED CORNER

Note the open area on the asphalt; it contains exploding pipes that will inflict serious damage if Batman gets too close! While proceeding up the street, a short cut-scene shows some goons running in and out of doorways just ahead. After the cut-scene, several thugs approach from three directions. Eliminate them using hand-to-hand combat, because there just isn't enough time to set up Batman's Batarang before they start shooting.

*Just like the pipe on the other street, this one will explode if Batman gets too close!*

*The enemy will move in and out of the doors on this street just before they attack.*

51

# GAZETTE SQUARE

After this last guy gets taken down, move to the double doors on the left side of the street.

If Batman gets knocked down, his excellent built-in counter-move will take down any nearby enemies. Have the Batcuffs ready to tie up the thugs as quickly as possible after knocking them down.

### ACT QUICKLY!
It's possible to get Batcuffs on a fallen foe even if other enemies are near as long as you act quickly. Notice in this screenshot that there is an enemy just behind Batman, but he will delay just long enough for the Batcuffs to be tied on!

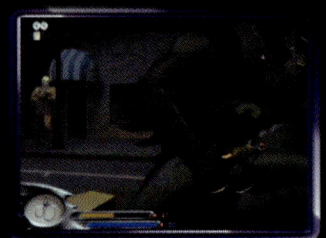

## THE BURNING CAFÉ

This isn't a mandatory area to explore, but the inside of the deli to the left of the street is on fire. Venture inside to extinguish the flames to come away with a **Sketchbook**! To enter the deli, go through the double doors. Be warned that once inside, a fire will

encircle Batman. Notice the panel on the wall? Use a Batarang (or punch it) to start the sprinkler system. After triggering the sprinklers, move around to the side of the room and pick up the **Sketchbook**.

Hitting the panel starts the water sprinklers.

To access the Sketchbook, the fire must be extinguished.

Kick down some boards to get out of the café once the fire is out.

# DELI DEBACLE

After snuffing out the café fire, move up the street toward the deli. Upon doing so, several thugs emerge. One particular thug emerges from the deli with a hostage! Use hand-to-hand combat to knock down and subdue the two enemies that open fire. Use the Batcuffs, then switch to the Batarang and aim it at the punk holding the hostage. If you get shot while trying to aim, the Batarang's First-Person View is reverted to the normal camera view. Aim the Batarang and, as soon as a blue locking signal appears, fire! The Batarang should subdue the enemy, thus enabling the hostage to go free.

*The thug emerges with his hostage.*

*Deal with the immediate threats first and the hostage-taker last.*

*Use the Batarang to take down the hostage-taker.*

There is a **Music CD** just past the deli entrance. It's tucked away at the end of the building. Don't forget to grab it before moving into the deli.

Inside the deli, don't hesitate for a second. Run directly forward and use super-kicks to knock out the two crooks. Apply the Batcuffs and the two remaining hoods in the store will be unable to shoot behind all the obstacles. After clamping down the first two thugs, run to the left and double-jump over the fallen shelves to tackle the guy in the corner. With this one restrained, the remaining enemy near the front window should be an easy target. If Batman's health is low, rejuvenate it with the Medical Kit, then head through the kitchen and out the back door to the next area—the Warehouse District!

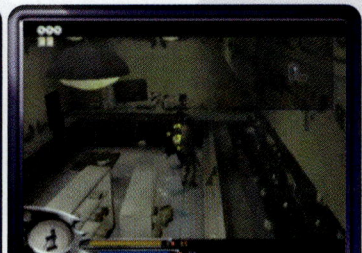
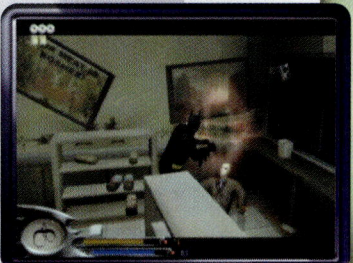
*There are four thugs in the deli. It's important to move through the entire area.*

*Next stop: the Warehouse District.*

# WAREHOUSE DISTRICT

HINTS:
THE UNIVERSAL TOOL CAN BE USED TO PICK LOCKS, OPEN VENTS, AND ACCESS COMPUTERS. RESTOCK YOUR SUPPLIES FROM THE WAYNE TECH BOXES.

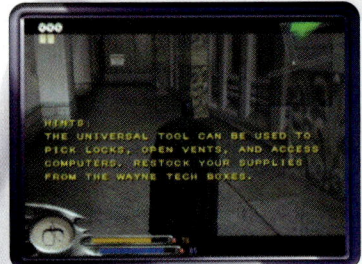

*Take the time to read the tips before moving onward.*

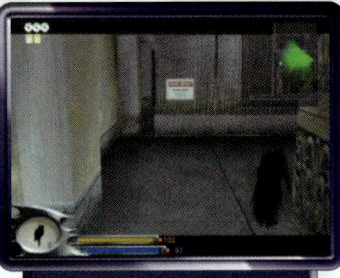

*Sneak up to this corner; don't rush toward it.*

Things are about to get much tougher—the Warehouse District is crawling with Black Mask's thugs, the False Face Society, who will quite literally be waiting around every corner! When approaching a corner or a blind alley, it's always best to enter Stealth Mode and slowly approach so that enemies aren't alerted. This area culminates in the battle with Black Mask himself!

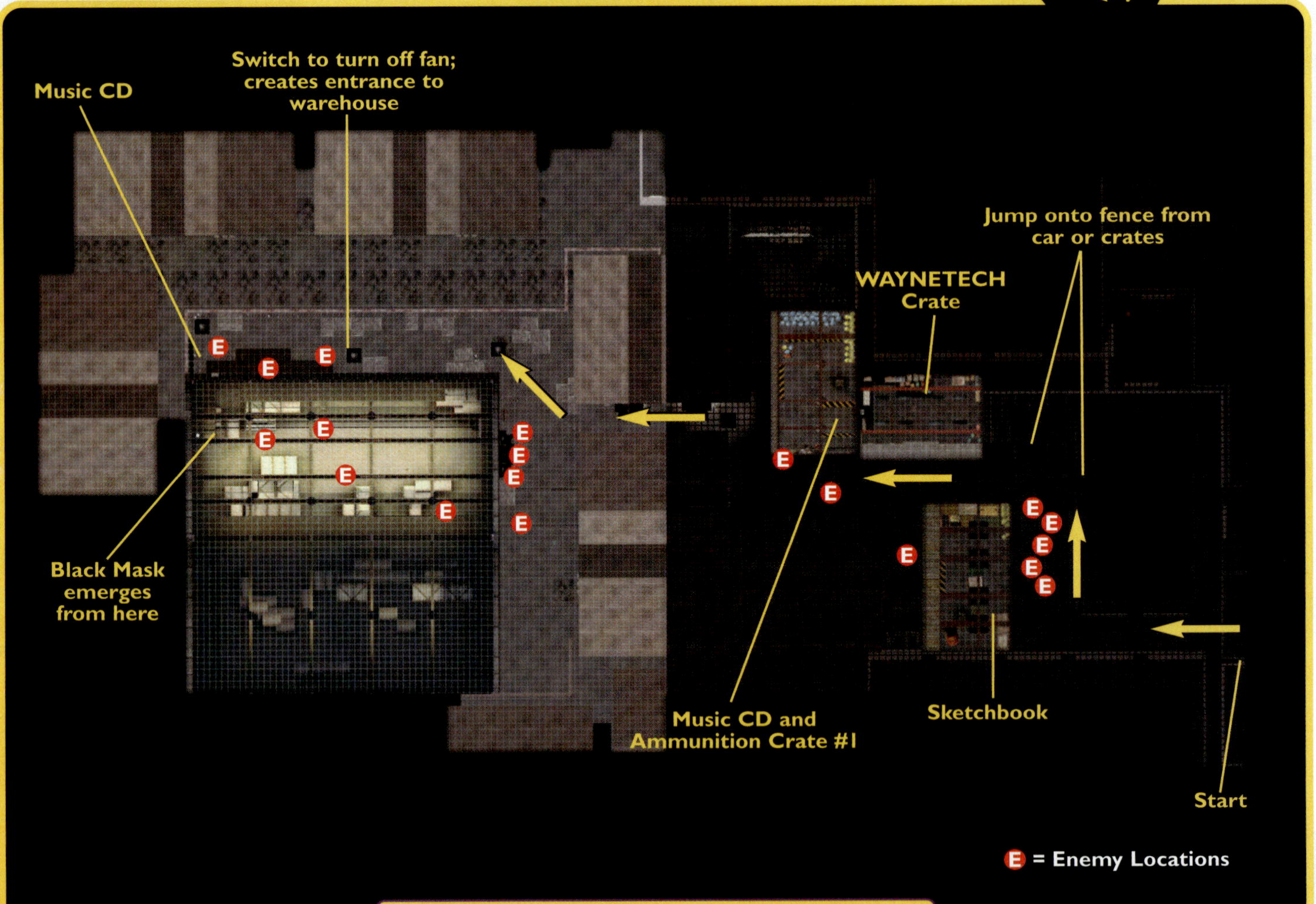

Music CD
Switch to turn off fan; creates entrance to warehouse
Jump onto fence from car or crates
WAYNETECH Crate
Black Mask emerges from here
Music CD and Ammunition Crate #1
Sketchbook
Start
E = Enemy Locations

WAREHOUSE DISTRICT

## FIVE-PACK

After walking into the Warehouse District, don't be in a hurry to run down the street. Instead, move up to the corner, press up against the wall, and use the corner view to target the four guards near the fence. Hit the guard in plain view using a Batarang; this action prompts the guards standing behind the cars to investigate. This provides an opportunity to knock out all four of guards with Batman's Batarangs, one at a time. If successful, rush over to the front of the gates and use Batman's Batcuffs on the bad guys.

*If the enemy gets too close, resort to hand-to-hand combat.*

### LOOK AROUND
Just because you throw a Batarang doesn't mean that it's gone forever! Oftentimes, they will bounce around an area, meaning you can simply walk over them to pick them back up. Perform a check for loose Batarangs after a battle to replenish any lost ones.

Because there are five enemies to fight in this area, it may prove easier to fight them in stages. What's likely to happen is that all of them will get knocked down, but there will be time to only cuff one or two of them before the others get up. If this occurs, knock them all out again and use the Batcuffs to tie up the stragglers! Use this tactic to restrain them all.

## JUMPING THE FENCE

The chain-link fence gate that leads to the next area is locked—even the Universal Tool won't work! To get across this fence, you must complete a special jump using the Bat Grapple. To do this, get up on top of the boxes and stand a short distance from the building. Send Batman's Bat Grapple up, then ascend the building. There are two ledges to attach to, but one is higher than the other.

Shoot for the higher ledge; if the ride up only goes a short distance, the Batarang latched onto the wrong ledge. Pull up and rotate to face the fence, then perform a flipping dismount. When done correctly, Batman will grab the top of the fence and pull himself up and over. This maneuver isn't difficult, but it may require a few attempts to get it right.

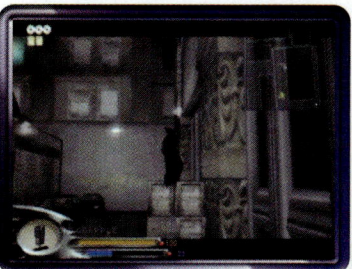
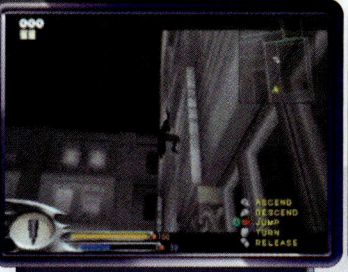

*Batman's position on the boxes is important.*

*The Bat Grapple enables Batman to ascend very high up the building.*

*Dismount to flip over the fence.*

55

# WAREHOUSE DISTRICT

*Attacking the first guy attracts the attention of nearby goons.*

## PARKING AREA & STORAGE ROOM

There is a great deal of resistance inside the Warehouse area. There are several enemies in the parking lot and inside the buildings. On more than one occasion, attacking a goon in the parking lot causes one or more of his buddies to emerge from inside a building. Start by moving around the corner to the left. Take out the thug but prepare to have at least two more show up (one from inside the building and another from the far parking lot).

After vanquishing the enemies, turn and use the Universal Tool to open the nearby door. There are some thugs inside hiding behind a storage container. Move quickly to silence them.

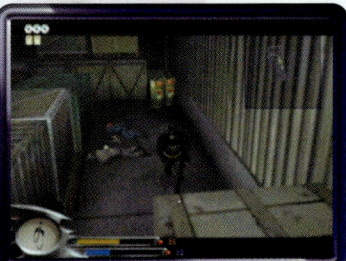

*The Universal Tool unlocks this door.*

*After disposing of the two guards, search the room for the hidden Sketchbook.*

Blow up these fuel drums by using a Batarang. After the explosion dies down, pick up the **Sketchbook** and move on!

## PARKING AREA & STORAGE ROOM

Exit the room and head back to the parking area. Note that there may or may not be one more False Face guard to take down (this depends on whether or not he was eliminated earlier). When the coast is clear, find another locked door and unlock it using the Universal Tool. This door leads to Room 2, which contains a much-needed WAYNETECH box that will rejuvenate Batman's health and weaponry.

There are a few items inside Room 2, but it's best to subdue the bad guys first. If the crooks aren't alerted to Batman's presence, walk up behind them and bang their heads together to take them both out at the same time. If not, they're still easy pickings because they likely won't sense Batman approaching. After properly disposing of them, go to the WAYNETECH box and replenish your supplies. There aren't any secret items in this area.

*Use the WAYNETECH box to replenish both health and equipment.*

# EXPLODING ENEMIES

Although you're getting closer to the whereabouts of Black Mask, there are some more guards to eliminate in the meantime. Move toward the unexplored area of the Warehouse District with caution. There are lots of thugs waiting at the end of the next section. For the most part, the majority of them are standing against the back wall—near some fuel drums! Use Batman's Batarang to blow up the fuel drums, then rush up and Batcuff all of the unconscious False Faces.

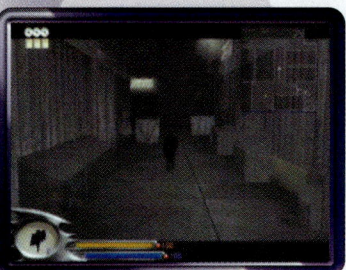

As you move through this area, you'll enter a new "section" of the Warehouse District.

Use a Batarang to detonate the fuel drums, thus destroying all the enemies in one fell swoop.

Explore the area if you want, but there's nothing of note nearby. Around the next corner is the stairway leading up to the Warehouse; this is where Black Mask is hiding out!

# GETTING AT BLACK MASK

After turning the corner, use the storage containers as cover to approach the enemy in relative safety. At the far end of this area (behind the staircase), locate the single fuel drum. Destroy it to find a **Music CD**. There is also a switch on the left side of the wall. Hit the switch to stop the fan and gain entry into the Warehouse.

Hit the switch on the wall to stop the ventilation fan. This enables you to enter the Warehouse where Black Mask is waiting.

Blow up the fuel drums behind the staircase, then get the **Music CD** hidden inside it.

Go through this fan area to enter the Warehouse.

After throwing the switch, the fan only stops for a few seconds before it automatically restarts, so you may have to hit the switch again after getting the Music CD. Charge up the stairs to reach the fan while it's still stopped, and ignore any warning cries from the guard above.

57

# WAREHOUSE DISTRICT

### FINISH THEM OFF!
There is a guard on a walkway above the stairs. To eliminate this threat, use the Bat Grapple to swing onto the ledge and take him out. This is not, however, necessary to do in order to fight Black Mask.

## THE CALM BEFORE THE STORM

Once safely inside the Warehouse, go into Stealth Mode and move to the left. Drop from the boxes to the floor, and take a moment to study the Bat Radar. The guard standing between the boxes scans the area in every direction rather swiftly. The two gangsters in the corner are members of the Scarface gang, who have been captured. If you want, climb back up on the crates and jump down on the guard between the boxes, or use a Batarang to take him out. Either way, it will likely alert two more guards who will quickly come running. Take them all down with a few power attacks.

Now run around and Batcuff the first three False Faces. The final guard won't emerge from behind the crates in the corner of the warehouse, even if he's alerted to Batman's presence. If he isn't alerted, then it's easy to sneak around one end or the other and put him in a sleeper hold. If the guard comes searching, charge around the crates and knock him down. After restraining all of the guards, Black Mask emerges.

*After taking down the three guards, use the Batcuffs on them. There's still one more guard to take down before Black Mask emerges.*

*With the final guard subdued, Black Mask appears and the battle commences.*

### ALTERNATE METHOD
As an alternate way to fight the guard *and* Black Mask, climb up the stairs and ladders and get on the support beams above the action. Knock off several of the boxes on the support beams to cause explosions, thus causing damage to those below. Beware, though, that once the guard spots Batman, he'll open fire!

# BLACK MASK

Before the fight begins, make Batman's Medical Kit the active belt item so that if his health reaches zero it will automatically replenish. When Black Mask appears, move close to him but stay behind the cover of the crates because he will start to shoot. Sneak behind him by moving around the left side of the crates (climb over them), then unleash a surprise attack. After initially engaging Black Mask, don't attempt to stand and fight with him or he'll pistol-whip and shoot Batman, depleting a great deal of health.

*Climb over these crates to get to Black Mask.*

The key to taking down Black Mask is to hit him hard, then immediately run away and hide behind a crate for a brief moment. Then emerge from behind the crate and perform a jumping spin-kick, then run and hide again. This technique is very effective because it eliminates Black Mask's powerful counter-attack, and it also takes away his ability to shoot with both of his pistols. On occasion, Black Mask will run to new locations in the Warehouse. When this occurs, follow him and continue the same pattern mentioned earlier. Don't, however, use the same pattern if Black Mask runs into an area with lots of fuel drums. If this happens, use Batman's Batarang and blow up one of the drums. This should set off a chain reaction that will damage him considerably.

*Rush him quickly and hit him hard.*

*When Black Mask goes down, get out of the way pronto or risk getting hit with a powerful counter-attack!*

## COUNTERACT THE LACK OF LIGHT

When Black Mask's health reaches about 50%, he'll shoot out the electrical box, thus dimming the lights even more. This doesn't have a profound effect, but if you have trouble seeing then use Batman's Night Vision goggles.

*If you get too close to Black Mask, he'll unleash a pistol-whip attack. This is a powerful attack, but don't give up—just get up and keep fighting.*

*Avoid a situation in which Black Mask starts pumping lead into Batman while he's on the ground.*

*This is the perfect situation. Safely hide between these boxes, run out and hit Black Mask, then return to the boxes!*

*Victory!*

# GOTHAM DOCKS

Now that Black Mask has been subdued, it's time to find Scarface. Fortunately, Oracle reveals that Scarface and his gang are at the Gotham Docks. The stakes continue to increase. It will take someone with extra sharp skills to make it through the docks alive. The Universal Tool and Night Vision goggles are needed to navigate through this dangerous area.

Good timing. I've just pinpointed Scarface's location. They're at--

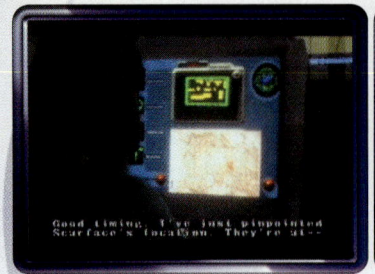

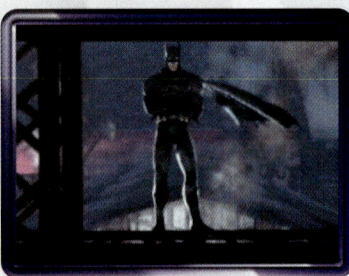

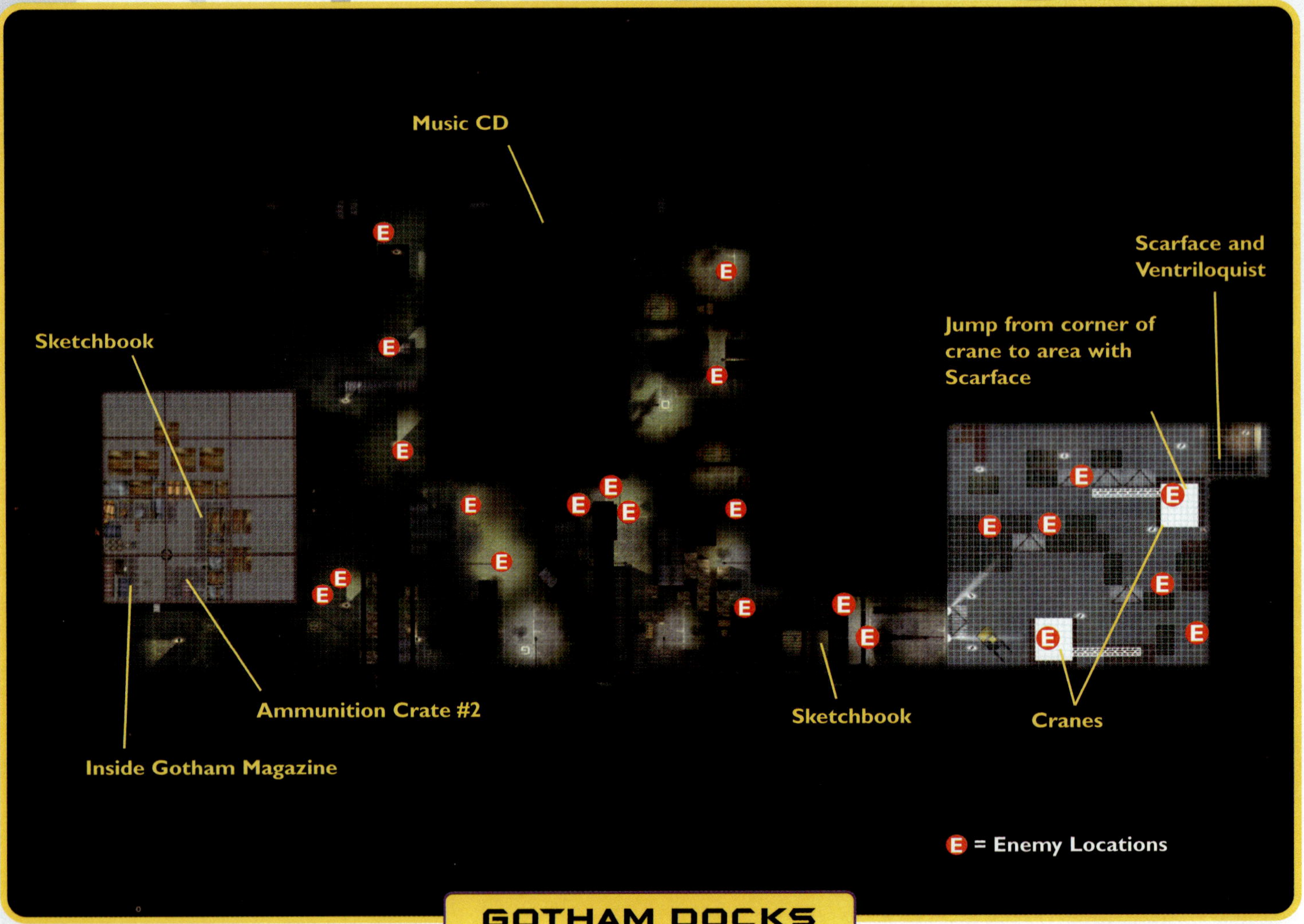
Music CD
Scarface and Ventriloquist
Sketchbook
Jump from corner of crane to area with Scarface
Ammunition Crate #2
Sketchbook
Cranes
Inside Gotham Magazine
E = Enemy Locations

GOTHAM DOCKS

# REFRESHMENTS

There are no enemies inside this room.

The Dock area, which is populated with Scarface's evil crew, is lined with dangerous laser traps so be wary upon entering the area. However, before you venture forth, use the Universal Tool to open the door to the left. Enter the room to find a WAYNETECH crate and replenish any dwindling supplies. Fully explore the area to find a **Sketchbook** and some other items.

To get the Sketchbook, blow up the fuel drums. After doing so, search the area for an **Inside Gotham Magazine** and an **Ammunition Crate**. After successfully clearing this area of all the goodies, head out into the night.

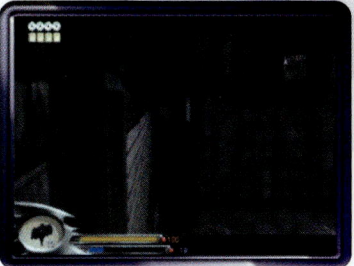

There is a copy of Inside Gotham Magazine in between the wall and this crate

Jump onto this crate to retrieve Ammunition Crate #2.

Blow up these fuel drums to reveal a Sketchbook.

### RESTOCKING SUPPLIES
WAYNETECH crates can be reused as many times as needed. So, if you take a beating from Scareface's thugs on the docks, return to one of these crates and replenish any lost supplies at the box.

## LASER-GUARDED DOCKS

Back on the docks, there are several problems that must be analyzed. Use Batman's Night Vision apparatus to see the laser trip-wires that are set up in and around the crates on the dock. Batman can easily climb over the boxes while in Stealth Mode, but it's better to fight the enemies and use the area's natural cover to make the job easier.

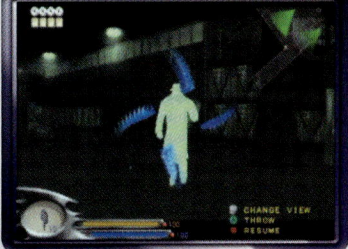

Use the Night Vision goggles to see the laser traps located on many of the crates.

Taking down the first enemy will likely stir the others, but cover is nearby.

Use the Batarang from the safety of the corner to take care of business.

# GOTHAM DOCKS

*There's one guard to take down in this area.*

After eliminating the first few enemies, rush over to them and Batcuff them as quickly as possible. After doing so, move to the left and head for the cover of the crates. There are no laser trip-wires in this area, and there's even a **Music CD** near the back.

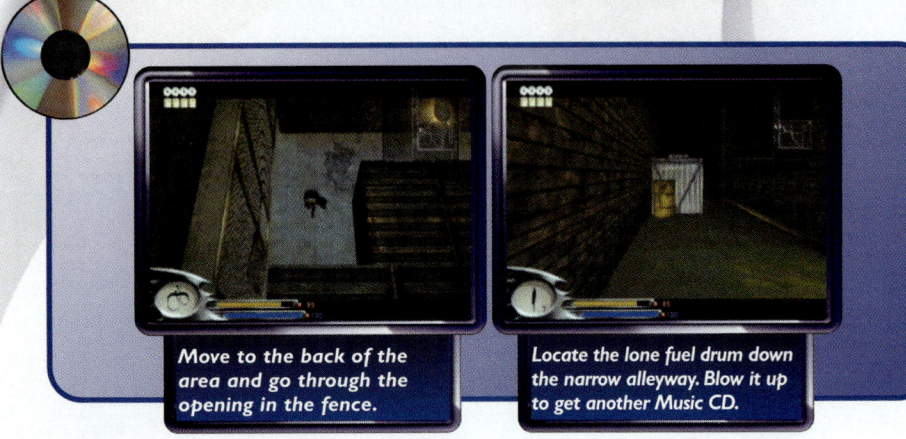

*Move to the back of the area and go through the opening in the fence.*

*Locate the lone fuel drum down the narrow alleyway. Blow it up to get another Music CD.*

Although it's possible to move down the narrow alleyway (past the location of the Music CD) to the other side of the docks, it's best to backtrack and go to the area where the laser traps are located.

## DEADLY DOCKS

Return to the area with the laser trip-wires on the crates. Go around the corner and attack any thugs in the area, but don't get too close to the fuel drums because the gunfire from the thugs could cause an explosion.

Alternatively, if you prefer to use a sneaky approach to fight the bad guys in this area, hop on top of the docks and use the fuel drums on the cargo crates to do the work instead. Push them off the crates to cause an explosion that will lay the enemies out flat!

### WARNING

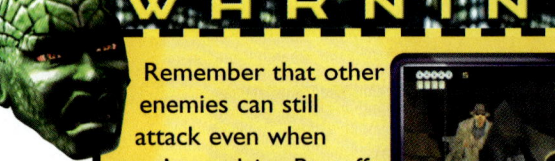

Remember that other enemies can still attack even when you're applying Batcuffs, like this thug who's coming up from behind!

The area that connects with the thin alleyway contains several exploding fuel drums. Sneak around the corner and use Batman's Batarang on these drums to avoid any hand-to-hand combat. The purpose of going through this area is strictly to get the **Sketchbook**.

**SKETCH BOOK** There's a **Sketchbook** in a crate in this area. The crate is in an open area, so kick the crate to retrieve the Sketchbook.

The last area before the dock cranes contains four of Scarface's men, all armed with machine guns. To dispose of these bad guys, climb the crates next to them and knock a fuel drum on top of them. This should take out three or four of them in one fell swoop, making the rest of the job much easier. Of course, hand-to-hand combat works just as well.

*Knocking this fuel drum off this crate can cause these enemies plenty of headaches, but it's a very safe option.*

*If you don't choose the "stealth" approach, fight these guys straight up.*

## THE DOCK CRANES

This is the final area before Scarface makes his appearance. The key to surviving this area is to get up the two dock cranes and take out the thugs manning them. If the crane operators aren't disposed of, they'll create havoc by swinging the giant crane hooks over nearly the entire area. Although there are also several enemies with guns in this area, the cranes are the first priority. After the cut-scene, run for the ladder that leads to the top of the crane and eradicate its operator.

  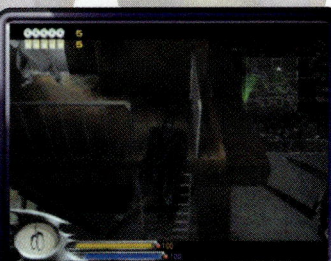 

*Upon entering the crane area, a cut-scene foretells of the danger coming.*

*Run straight to the ladder, then climb up and take this guy out!*

# PRELUDE

**WARNING**

If you don't dispose of the crane operator quickly enough, he will start swinging the heavy crane hook. It's extremely difficult to avoid getting hit by it. The hook will diminish about one-third of Batman's health each time it connects.

After securing the crane, jump down and remove the two gang members. Lock them up with the Batcuffs, then run toward the second crane and do the same thing as noted earlier. Again, time is of the essence here; delay too long before climbing the ladder, and the crane operator will unleash the giant hook.

Use the Batcuffs on these guys, then destroy the second crane.

**TRY THIS**

You can leave this area from the second crane by jumping where Scarface is hiding. This can be accomplished right after you dispose of the second crane operator. In short, you don't have to disable and Batcuff the entire gang to move on. In fact, there are no more items or secrets here, so you can end it right now by jumping.

It's not necessary to cuff them, but there are still three more thugs wandering about. Clear them out of the area, go back up the crane, and jump down into Scarface's hiding place. This triggers a cut-scene in which Batman silences Scarface, while Robin and Batgirl show up to polish off the job. Now it's off to the Talbot Factory.

    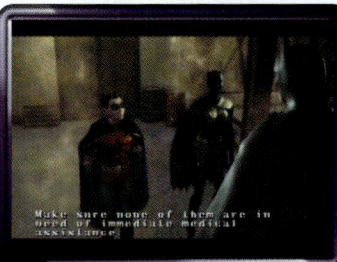

There are still a few enemies kicking around the docks.

From the back-right corner of the crane, jump down onto Scarface.

# TALBOT FACTORY

After a brief chat with the Commissioner's underlings, scale the side of the building to get to his office.

Oracle reveals that her father, the Commissioner, has disappeared and there are no clues to his whereabouts. First, go to the Gotham City Police Department rooftop to assess the situation, then explore the Commissioner's office. The trail leads to the abandoned Talbot Factory, where you'll undoubtedly have your hands full!

- Sketchbook
- Work Release Form 2A
- Exit through vent
- Use Universal Tool to open door
- Exit to Underground Sewers
- Sketchbook
- Music CD
- Start
- **E** = Enemy Locations

**TALBOT FACTORY**

6 5

# TALBOT FACTORY

## GETTING TO THE COMMISSIONER'S OFFICE

After a chat with the Commissioner, Batman stands perched on a ledge on the side of the GCPD building. The entry into the office is on the far side of the building, two stories below the starting point. To get down there, drop to the left side ledge, turn and drop to the right side ledge, then do it all again to reach the proper level. Move down (away from the camera) to find the open window.

Move toward the window to automatically move inside.

## OUTSIDE THE TALBOT FACTORY

The trail leads to the abandoned Talbot Factory. Unfortunately, the Talbot Factory isn't exactly empty, and its inhabitants, a street gang known as the Dregs, are focused on only one thing: Batman's demise. There are four foes to fight right away. If possible, use a Batarang to take down at least two of the thugs, because the fighting will be tough. The large guy with the baseball bat is particularly difficult to handle.

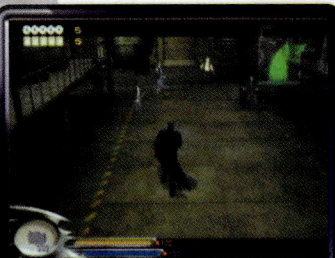
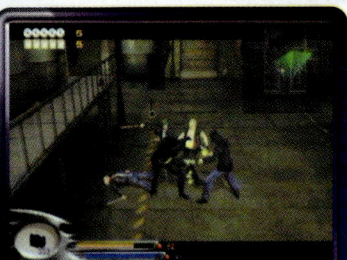

It's very easy to get pummeled if you're not careful.

### GETTING YOUR PRIORITIES STRAIGHT
The large thug with the bat and the vest gets up more quickly than the others when he gets knocked down, so it's a good idea to Batcuff him first.

There is a **Music CD** along the side of the piping.

There are two more enemies guarding the doorway to the factory, but they are relatively easy to eliminate with a Batarang or hand-to-hand combat. With these thugs removed from action, enter the factory.

# THE FACTORY FLOOR

There are some fuel drums inside the factory. In fact, some of the bad guys are using them as cover. Blow up the fuel drums to knock out the thugs, then do some Batcuffing!

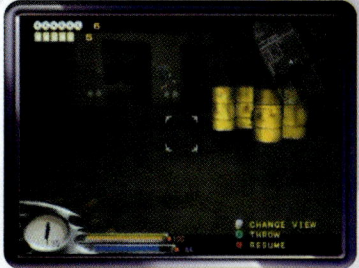
It looks rather tame initially, but there are thugs behind these fuel drums.

Use Batman's Batarang to ignite the fuel drums in the area.

There are lots of enemies in the Factory Floor area. There are three behind the drums, a couple more on the catwalk above, and two more inside the gear that sprawls across the back of the room. As if that isn't enough, two enemies emerge from the back room. Move around and clear the room of this enemy infestation. Along the way, search for a **Sketchbook** and a **Work Memorandum**.

Even the bad guy up top must be cuffed.

Don't worry about getting hung up in the machinery; you can hop through all of it.

In this screenshot, Batman is standing near the Sketchbook's location.

Move into the room at the back and clear out the thugs inside, then pick up the **Work Memorandum** on the desk. With the enemy threat out of the way, cruise the area one more time to ensure that it is free of enemies. To leave, move to the ventilation shaft and hop up.

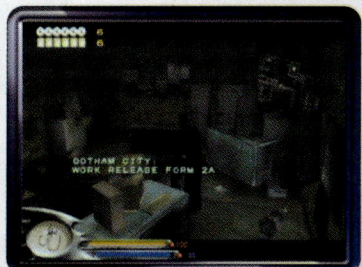
This tidbit of information indicates how to get to the sewers.

## FINDING THE SEWERS

The storage room is guarded by two bad guys. Since Batman is behind them, use a Batarang or sneak up and take them down by using hand-to-hand combat. Use the Universal Tool on the door to continue.

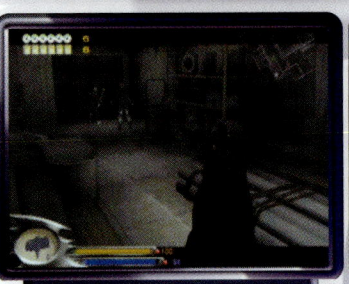 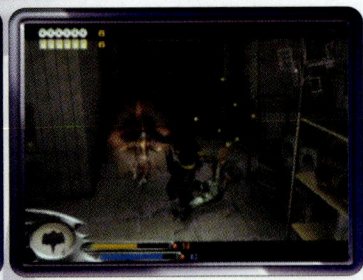 

*Use the element of surprise in this situation.*

## ELECTRICAL ROOM

This room leads down to the Underground Sewers. It's best to stay away from the Sewer entrance (in the far corner of the room) before picking up the **Sketchbook** hidden inside the fuel drum. After acquiring the Sketchbook, move down through the portal into the Underground Sewers.

**SKETCH BOOK**

*The Sketchbook is inside this drum.*

# UNDERGROUND SEWERS

The time has come to enter the dark recesses of the Underground Sewers. Although the overhead map of the sewers looks imposing and overwhelming, the path through the Underground Sewers is linear. There are, of course, several areas that you don't need to explore (if you don't want to pick up all of the items), but this walkthrough indicates each item's location to make things easier. The sewers are a tough place because the enemies are abundant and the confined spaces can make escaping somewhat difficult.

### UNDERGROUND SEWERS

- Start
- Sketchbook
- Break through wall here
- Set switches to: Up, Down, Up (from left to right)
- Music CD (use Bat Cable to reach)
- Electrified water
- Sketchbook
- Water valve
- Equipment replenishment room
- Entrance to Arkham Asylum
- Sketchbook
- Music CD
- Ratcatcher boss fight
- Bitten pipe
- E = Enemy Locations

# UNDERGROUND SEWERS

## FIVE ON ONE

Once in the sewers area, there is only one path to take: toward the T intersection. While approaching this junction, two thugs suddenly appear and, as if that isn't enough, three more quickly follow. Quickly dispose of them and use Batman's Batcuffs to subdue them all.

*Batcuff these bad guys, then continue to explore the area.*

Make a right at the T intersection, then look for the first left turn. Although the path is currently blocked, don't let it fool you—there's a Sketchbook to uncover here. If you're not looking for it, it's easy to run right past it.

*There's a Sketchbook to the left in this hallway.*

## THE BROKEN WALL

Proceed down the hallway to another left turn. This one leads down to a water puddle with electrical wires in it. Don't explore the path straight ahead; the only thing in this area are the Dregs.

*Around the corner is nothing but a dead end.*

The goal is to get past the area with the electrical wires. It's safe to assume that stepping in the water causes significant damage (nearly one-third of a full health bar). With this in mind, jump to the concrete platform on the left and jump past it to the hallway just beyond. The large room is guarded by a group of tough enemies. Break out the Batarang and take some of them out before they get too close. Batcuff each one as quickly as possible.

*These guys will quickly attack.*

*Falling into the water causes significant damage.*

*It's a brawl in this area!*

70

### USE THE ENVIRONMENT TO YOUR ADVANTAGE

Examine the area and locate the fuel drums, then use them to destroy the enemies in the large room. If you have a spare Batarang, put it to good use!

*Punch out the wall, then move through the opening.*

When the coast is clear, move around the back of the large room to find the dead end. Look closely to find an area that looks slightly cracked and broken.

## TIME FOR A DIP

Move down the hallway and keep an eye open for some thugs who emerge from the two hallways on the left. These guys are tough and more of them appear when the fight begins, so work quickly! There are no goodies down either of the side passages, so keep moving straight ahead. At this point, the area appears to end in a dead end. All you need to do to bypass the area is walk right up to it and swim underneath the cave-in.

*Work quickly, then move on.*

*When you reach the dead end, just keep walking and Batman automatically submerges.*

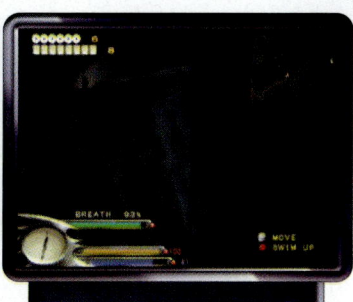
*While underwater, turn left and surface.*

## SEWER CENTRAL

After emerging from the water, move straight down the corridor to the small tube on the left. Move through the tube to access the next area. Now go down the hallway to the central Sewer area. This area has several sewer corridors that are closed off, and there are three sets of switches in one corner that open the corridors. Set the switches by hitting the left switch and the right switch (don't touch the middle switch). Pressing these switches opens the only exit. Hitting the other switches unlocks the other areas, but there are no items there and you *will* let three crocodiles into the central pond! Therefore, it's highly recommended that you avoid the crocodiles all together.

*This central room has three switches (to the left in this screenshot) that control the gates to the exits.*

*Set the switches like this.*

*This is the exit. After setting the switches (1 and 3), move down this corridor.*

*When you get to this door, take it.*

# UNDERGROUND SEWERS

## THE SECRET UNDERGROUND WAREHOUSE

There are a bunch of rooms to go through to get to the next area of the Underground Sewers. After a brief chat with Oracle, switch to Batman's Night Vision goggles to see a doorway. It's in a sunken room full of water and electrical wires. You can't open the door until the water is gone, so move through the door and go down the stairs to the left. Take off the Night Vision goggles for now.

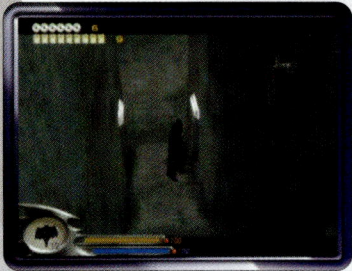
The door is visible while using the Night Vision goggles, but the water must be drained from the room to open the door.

Head down the stairs.

There are two doors at the bottom of the stairs. Take the one on the right. Inside this room is a pipe with a valve on it. Close the valve (this stops the water in the room upstairs), then proceed back upstairs and use the Night Vision goggles to open the secret door. Take this opportunity to stock up on items. Do so now, because the Ratcatcher is about to make an appearance!

After draining the water, use the Night Vision goggles to open the door.

Backtrack down the stairs back to the two doors, but take the left door this time. This leads to a small room with a fuel drum on one side and a door on the other. Blow up the fuel drum to obtain a **Sketchbook**, then take the door out and back into the sewers.

The Sketchbook is inside this fuel drum.

## THE WATERFALL ROOM

After heading back out into the Sewers, there's only one way to go and it leads directly to the Waterfall Room where three sewer pipes converge. The task is to go down the pipe to the right, but there's no direct way to get to it. The area directly across contains a **Music CD** that looks tantalizing, but it's not particularly easy to reach. Start by jumping down into the pool, then swim over to the slab of concrete sticking out of the water between (and below) the two other sewer pipes.

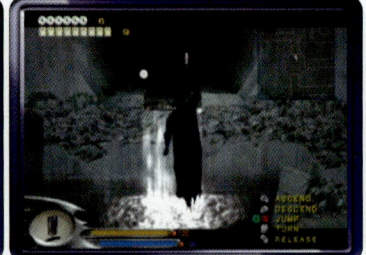
Although you can Bat Grapple right to the Music CD, you can't get it this way.

Use the Bat Grapple here to go up.

*From here, jump to the exit ledge.*

*Move down the exit pipe to leave this area.*

Use the Bat Grapple to access the exit ledge, then use the Bat Cable to swing over and get the **Music CD**. Use the Bat Grapple again to return to the exit ledge after obtaining the Music CD. Now go back to the exit pipe and run down to the small tube exit on the left, then hop inside.

*Swing right into the Music CD while using the Bat Cable.*

## RATS!

This area is infested with rats. A different strategy is needed to defeat these creatures. The rats are very resilient and will come back to fight again and again, so keep moving and don't stand still when fighting.

*The rats keep coming, so kick them to clear the way and keep moving!*

**WARNING**
The rats just keep coming in this area, so kick them and get moving. If not, Batman will take too many unnecessary hits.

*Kick the crate to reveal a Music CD.*

# UNDERGROUND SEWERS

Keep moving through the rooms (don't pass by the **Sketchbook** inside the crate), but beware of the rats. As a general rule, jumping is a good way to avoid them. A powerful kick will also do the trick, but don't get bogged down in fighting the Rats—just keep moving!

Climb the stairs and go through the next door to find the Ratcatcher!

Kick open another crate to find a Sketchbook.

## RATCATCHER

You don't actually fight the Ratcatcher one-on-one. Instead, this boss sends a pair of his specially bred beauties after Batman. These giant rats stick close to the ground, so punches won't inflict much damage. Instead, kicks will inflict big time damage to these dastardly creatures.

Equip the Batarang and hit the giant rats as many times as possible. As the rats draw near, kick them a few times and jump to avoid their attacks. It's important to ensure that *both* creatures don't attack simultaneously. If they manage to do so, it causes a lot of damage. Focus on eliminating one of the rats entirely; it's much easier to fight them one at a time.

When the rats approach, hit one of them because the one that gets hit will generally turn and run. This ensures that you only fight one rat at a time. It's also important to equip a Medical Kit at the start of the fight. After depleting both rats of their health, the battle ends.

# ARKHAM ASYLUM
## PART ONE

Now that the Ratcatcher is in custody, it's time to rise up out of the sewers and head to the Arkham Asylum. Hopefully, the answers to the question of who's behind everything will be answered within the walls of Gotham's premiere mental health facility.

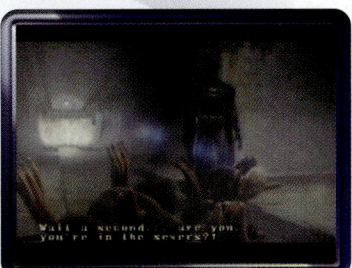

- Dr. McKee locked in Killer Croc's cell
- Water valve
- Throw the switch here
- Killer Croc cell key
- Throw switch here
- Sketchbook
- Music CD
- Music CD
- Exit
- Enter Here
- Personal Notes
- Start
- E = Enemy Locations

**ARKHAM ASYLUM**

## ENTER THE ASYLUM

After the communication with Robin ends, pass through a couple of doors and climb some stairs out of the sewers. Batman should emerge near a large oval door that leads to the Arkham Asylum. Enter at your own risk, because the inscription on the door reads "Abandon all hope, ye who enter."

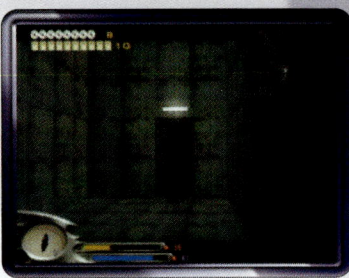  

The Arkham Asylum is through these doors.

## THE BATTLE WITH INSANITY

The situation in the Asylum is one of chaos, with most or all of the inmates roaming freely around the Asylum halls armed with clubs and other weaponry. Dispose of all inmates in this initial area, and make sure all of them get Batcuffed, too. Note that some enemies are hiding behind corners, plus there are one or two items to pick up.

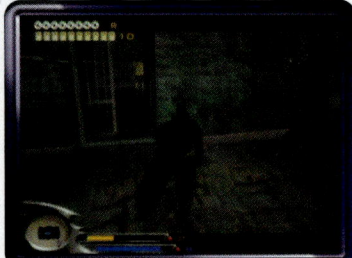   

Continue straight down the hallway and these bad guys will come looking for a fight.

Pick up anything in the area, like this Memorandum.

### WARNING

Several of the inmates hide around corners, awaiting the prime opportunity to launch an ambush attack. Be ready for sneak attacks!

## THE INSANITY CONTINUES...

Move past the gate and venture into the next area (a load screen appears when you do this). The next hallway is crowded with four or five inmates. Take them all down quickly and Batcuff them. Don't enter the room to the left just yet; focus on eliminating the enemies first.

It's a brawl in this area.

After securing the hallway, enter the room on the left (as you entered the hallway). There are three tough and vicious inmates inside, but Batman can dispose of them with a few powerful kicks and punches. WARNING: A fourth inmate will pop out of one of the boxes in the room. After successfully restraining the thugs, kick the crate to find a **Music CD**. Then use a Batarang to blow up the fuel drums. This reveals a **Sketchbook** to add to your burgeoning collection.

There's a Music CD inside the crate.

The Sketchbook is inside the drums.

## ACTIVATE THE DOOR

There are two automatic doors on the right-hand side of the hallway. To open these doors, walk to the end of the hallway and use the Universal Tool on the door to open it. Once it's open, enter the room and hit the switch.

The switch has been activated once the light turns green.

## CLEARING THE CELLS

Move through this open gate, and note the water on the ground. Killer Croc must be free!

Move toward the first door in the hallway (on the way back from the control room). The door automatically opens, revealing a club-wielding inmate who must be subdued. Once that is accomplished, proceed cautiously back down the hallway—there are inmates everywhere.

# ARKHAM ASYLUM

Upon reaching the cell area, take note of the pooling water on the ground. Move down the cellblock and take out the inmates. Enter the hallway and watch the cut-scene, which reveals that Killer Croc has locked a doctor in his cell.

# KILLER CROC

Killer Croc locks Batman into a half-flooded room. The water will prevent Batman from executing some of his moves in his arsenal. Specifically, the ability to kick and jump is significantly reduced. The key to defeating Killer Croc is to get in close and hit him with a continuous barrage of punches to keep him off balance.

Killer Croc will grab Batman and push him under the water. When this occurs, press the buttons on your controller to break away from his grasp. If Batman gets knocked down, use a leg-sweep counterattack to cause some damage to Croc. Remember to keep a Medical Kit active to revive Batman if his health reaches zero.

*If Croc holds Batman under water for more than a few seconds, his breath will drain to zero.*

If Batman gets submerged for a short period of time, return to the other side of the room and stay away from Croc for a while to quickly recover. Don't immediately engage in fighting with Croc soon after a "dunking" occurs; if you do so, Batman likely won't survive a second "dunking."

Get into a punching rhythm and hammer away at Croc constantly; this should prevent him from counterattacking. It's not vitally important to knock down Killer Croc, because he can perform a leg-sweep counterattack while down. This then gives him time to get up and prepare for the next attack. Attack with regular punches at close range to make it more difficult for him to recover.

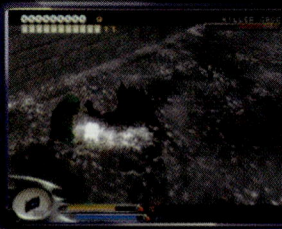

*A barrage of short punches like this will take down Croc faster than fancy combos.*

# OBTAIN THE KEY CARD

Now there are three things to do. First, stop the flow of water into the area. Second, get the key to Killer Croc's cell off his body. Third, talk to the doctor to get her Key Card security pass so that you can access the upper levels of the Asylum. The water shutoff is just outside the room where you fought Killer Croc. Turn the valve to disengage it, then search Croc for the key.

The Key is on Croc's body.

Replenish items while inside this room.

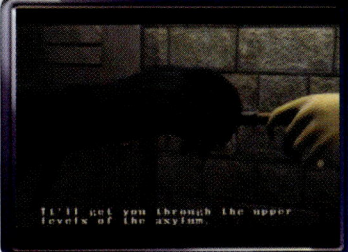

Return to Killer Croc's cell with the Cell Key and open the door. It turns out that the prisoner is Dr. McKee. She explains that all of the prisoners appear to be loose, including the Joker, but she knows nothing of Commissioner Gordon's whereabouts. Take the Key Card from her and move on!

## THE NEXT LEVEL

With the Key Card in your possession, go to the other areas of the Asylum. Move back down the hallway (explore the cells if you want) and go past the automatic door into the original hallway. Turn the corner to the other automatic door and enter it. There's another inmate inside—take him down! Move down the hallway and take a left at the T intersection. Walk to the room at the far end of this hallway and throw the switch inside. The next door takes you to the second level of the Asylum.

Move around to the other automatic door.

Enter this room with caution—there are two thugs inside.

Throw this switch, then move back to the other side of the T intersection.

# ARKHAM ASYLUM
## PART TWO

You got a taste for what's in store while in Arkham Asylum, but things are about to get much, much stickier! In a short while, Mr. Freeze and Poison Ivy make an appearance, so be prepared. The hallways of Arkham Asylum quickly become tangled with reams of foliage, courtesy of Poison Ivy. The vines not only cover the walls, but they also attack!

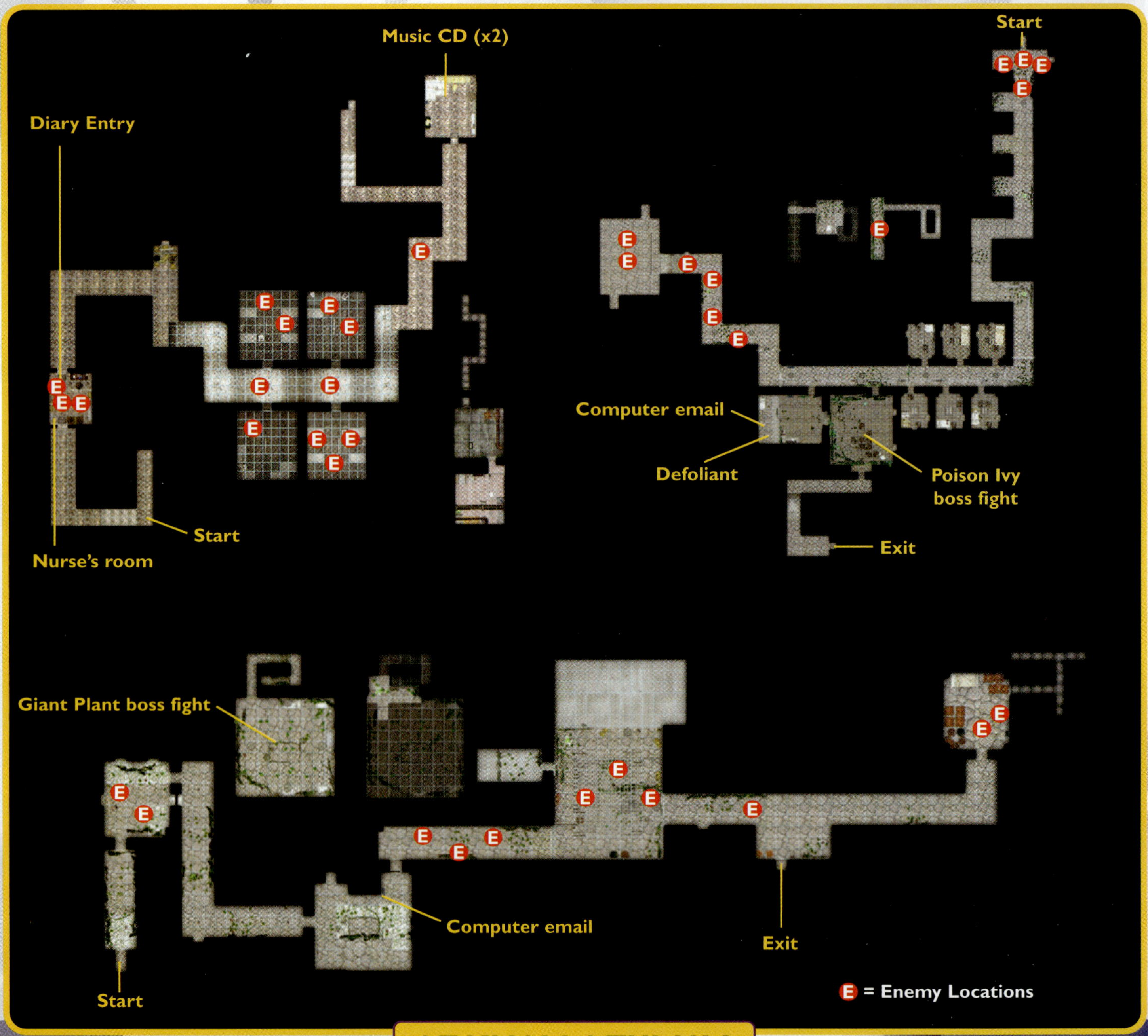

## FREE THE NURSES

Use the new Pass Key to get past the door. Note the crate just inside the door; smash it to get a **Music CD**. After doing so, climb the stairs to reach the hallway above. This triggers the sound of female voices crying out for help.

Grab the Music CD inside the crate just before the stairs.

While moving up the stairs, voices warn that there are inmates loose. Go through the door and enter the room. Take out the two inmates and bind them, then pick up the **Diary Entry** off the desk. To leave the room, crouch down directly in front of the nurses and press the Action button. You must be in just the right place for this to happen. After talking to them, open the door to continue the quest.

There are two nurses and a pair of inmates through this door.

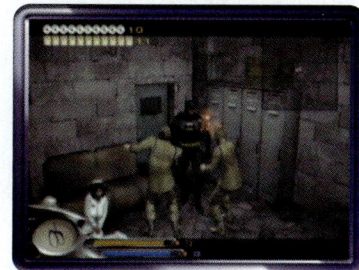

The Diary Entry says a lot about Arkham.

## CLEAR THE CELL BLOCK

The next set of hallways leads to a cell block that contains four cells. While none of these cells contain any items, each one has inmates that must be defeated. Move down the halls and take down any inmates. Once at the cell block, there are three or four inmates to fight and each cell has another pair of thugs!

Plenty of fighting occurs around the cell block.

Some of the inmates often hide behind curtains in the cells.

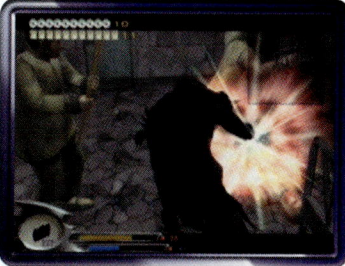

Two of the cells have three enemies in them, and they will attack all at once!

# ARKHAM ASYLUM

## ITEMS

Past the Cell Block there are several more enemies to eliminate. Clear them out and move to the room at the end of the hallway. There is an inmate hiding inside a box in this room, but there's also a pair of **Music CDs** to find after blowing up the fuel drums!

Move up the stairs to access Poison Ivy's area.

This is the first Music CD.

The second one is on the other side of the room.

## THE GREEN HALLS OF HOME

Up the stairs is a rather tropical-looking area that has obviously been influenced by Poison Ivy's touch. The walls are covered with foliage, but don't be fooled by this serene setting. In fact, the foliage will drop sacs of poison as you walk past! After a short cut-scene, dispose of the inmates guarding the room, then look for the exit on the far side of the room.

Things immediately become clear when you enter Poison Ivy's domain.

A Sketchbook is inside the drums.

Upon entering the next hallway, it becomes obvious why Poison Ivy is so dangerous. The plant hanging off the walls will drop poison sacs onto the floor. Move down the hall to the next door.

### EVADING THE POISON GAS

The green clouds of poison gas are extremely dangerous to Batman's health, so when a sac drops to the ground move past it quickly. If one drops in front of you, stay put and let the cloud dissipate before moving on.

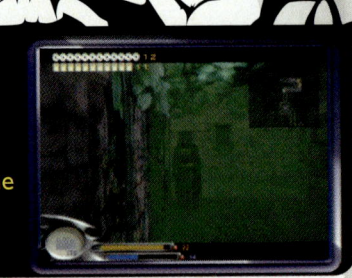

82

## SAVE THE GUARD

Pass through the next door to find a guard entangled by some of Poison Ivy's plant matter. Since he's blocking the pathway, you must save him to continue. Go through the doorway and down the stairs into the area below.

Upon entering the room below, Batman comes face-to-face with a giant plant that wants nothing more than to destroy him. There's only one way to take this plant out and that's to fight it!

# PLANT CREATURE

The Giant Plant has long vines that will lash out and cause significant damage. For the most part, it's difficult to avoid taking a few hits—just accept that it's going to happen!

To eliminate the Giant Plant, get close to it and repeatedly kick it until it falls over. Punches or combos also work, but as a rule of thumb, you need to connect with four or five good kicks (the kind that yield a red halo) to destroy it. Don't waste any time with finesse, just move straight in and attack aggressively!

The Giant Plant also drops poison sacs.

When the plant slumps over, move back upstairs and talk to the guard.

## CLEAR THE AREA

Once the guard is safe, he says that there's some Defoliant at the guard station at the end of the hallway. Your task is to make it to the station and obtain the Defoliant for the upcoming battle with Poison Ivy. Before doing so, however, pick up the hardcopy of the computer email on the ground, then continue down the hallway. After passing through the door, more inmates come down the hallway; use Batman's Batarang to silence them.

Pick up the email on the ground.

Now is the perfect time to use a Batarang.

# ARKHAM ASYLUM

Move down the hall to the cell block covered with foliage. Use the Bat Grapple (or just jump up) to swing up to the upper level of this area. Take out the enemies and keep moving. Be advised that more poisonous sacs will drop while proceeding down the hallway.

*There's actually nothing up here but a doorway that comes into play later.*

*Move around to the other automatic door.*

Move to the very end of the hall and take out the guards inside the room, then move back to the doorway leading down to the next level.

*Enter this room with caution; there are several inmates inside.*

## GOING DOWN

Find the doorway on the side wall that leads down to the next level. At the bottom of the stairs, locate the long corridor with lots of doors. There's also a large group of inmates that will attack. Keep a Medical Kit handy to heal any damage sustained during this fight.

*It's a very tough fight in this area.*

Now move to the door on the left and descend the staircase. At the bottom of the stairs, a lone inmate has fallen on the ground. Use the Batcuffs on him, then move back upstairs.

## FINDING POISON IVY

Move down the hallway with caution past the opened gate (watch out for more poison sacs). Continue to the second open gate, but pause a moment to let the cloud of poison gas dissipate.

*Let the gas dissipate before moving on.*

There are four cells to explore in this area. Some of them contain inmates, but there are no items to find in any of them. Clear the area and head for the doorway on the left side of the hall. This door leads to Poison Ivy! Pick up the email and **Defoliant** inside the room. Suddenly, Poison Ivy breaks through the wall and attacks!

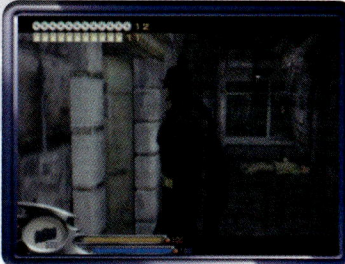

This door leads to Poison Ivy!

Grab the email.

The Defoliant is on the table.

Uh oh!

# PLANT MONSTER

Poison Ivy's giant plant is a large stalk that sits at the back of the room. It releases poison gas and lashes out with large jaws on the end of its tentacles. The key to victory is to get close to the stalk and hit it repeatedly. Don't get into a fight with the tentacles; this only makes the fight more difficult. Rush in quickly and get beyond the tentacles, then hammer away!

If Batman takes a hit or gets poisoned, try to move back in close to the stalk and continue to hit it. Punches are effective, but kicks tend to inflict more damage.

She's been waiting for you...

It's game over for Poison Ivy—for now!

# ARKHAM ASYLUM
## PART THREE

With Poison Ivy back in custody, three main enemies remain in the Arkham Asylum: Mr. Freeze, Zsasz, and The Joker. Hmmm… It's beginning to look like the Joker isn't behind this after all!

After leaving the room, continue through the open gate and around the corner to the right.

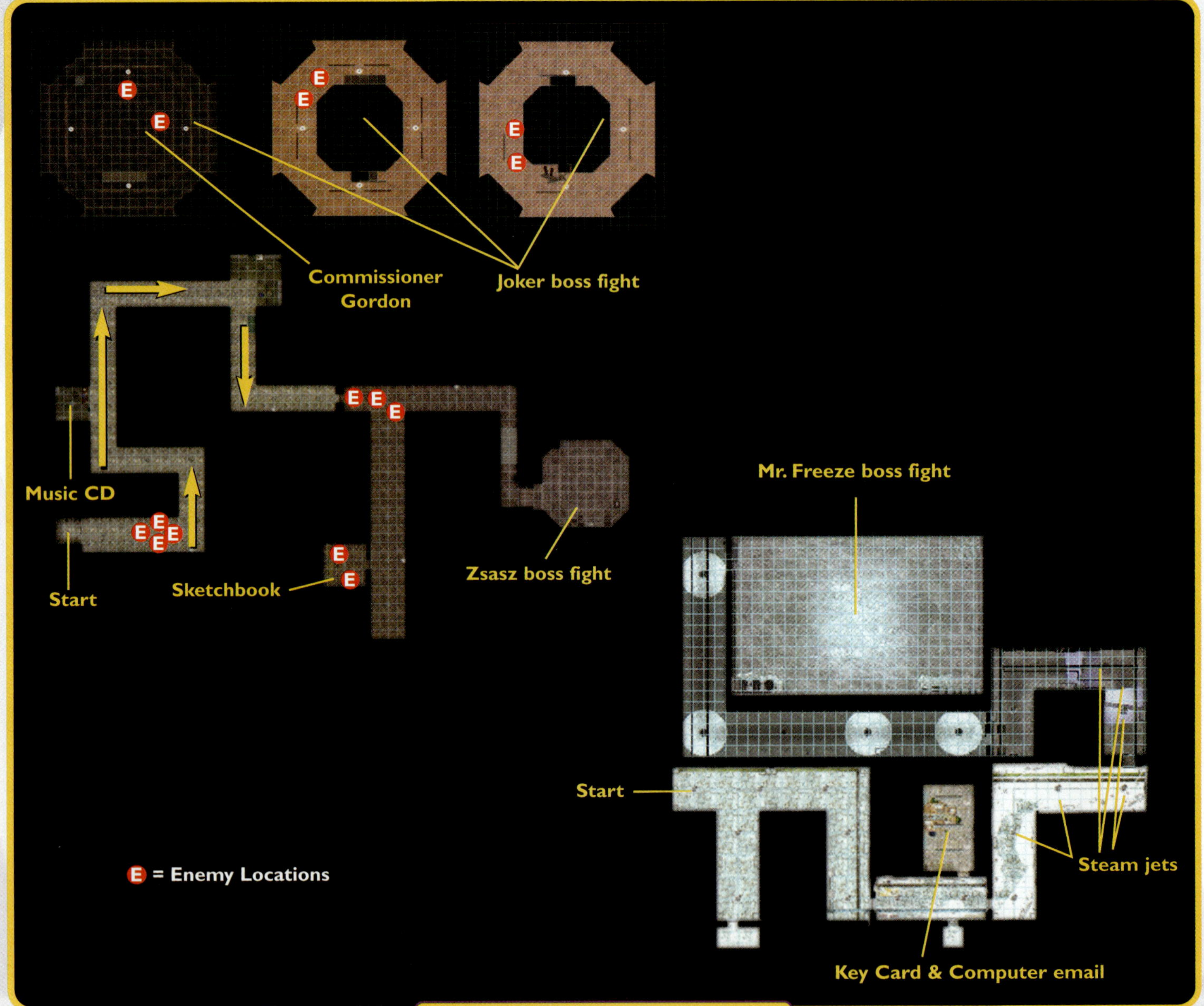

- Commissioner Gordon
- Joker boss fight
- Music CD
- Start
- Sketchbook
- Zsasz boss fight
- Mr. Freeze boss fight
- Start
- Key Card & Computer email
- Steam jets

**E** = Enemy Locations

**ARKHAM ASYLUM**

*It's not necessary to mop up these inmates, but it's nice to ensure that they're all gone before moving on.*

## MOP UP

Dispose of any remaining inmates wandering around the hallways beyond Poison Ivy's room, then return to the room where you defeated Poison Ivy.

## INTO THE COLD

Find the unlocked door inside the room where Poison Ivy is tied up, then climb the stairs to locate another door. This one, however, requires a Pass Key to enter. After opening the door, it becomes readily apparent that this is Mr. Freeze's territory. Move through this part of the Asylum from area to area. There aren't any inmates around, so just move carefully and keep your eyes open.

*This door opens without a Pass Key.*

After exploring the area, move out and go through the only other door available. Beware of multiple steam blasts in this area; avoid them to prevent any unnecessary damage. A double-jump is the best way to clear the steam without taking a hit. Go through the door to enter a long rectangular room. There is a silver door on the left side of the room (the sign reads "Authorized Personnel Only" on it). Ignore it for now, but keep its location in mind for later.

*Perform a double-jump to get over the steam blasts.*

## MEET MR. FREEZE

Move through the reddish door at the end of the room and jump over the blasts of steam. Travel down the hallways and move through the doors. Eventually, you will reach a room with a large freezer that runs the entire expanse of the right wall. Move to the end of this area and go through the door to meet Mr. Freeze face-to-face!

*Mr. Freeze awaits.*

# MR. FREEZE

Mr. Freeze has several attacks, the most annoying of which is his freeze ray. The freeze ray will completely freeze Batman's feet, stopping him dead in his tracks for a short period of time. Jumping is an excellent way to avoid this attack. Also, he only periodically attacks with the freeze ray.

Although spin kicks and power attacks will knock down Mr. Freeze, these attacks enable him to compose himself for his next attack. It's best to get close to Mr. Freeze and hit him with several punches or kicks in succession. This should quickly deplete his hit points and it will prevent him from unleashing too many counter-attacks.

Mr. Freeze is *very* slow, which works to your advantage. This creates an opportunity to move and jump around him with ease, which makes it easier to avoid his freeze ray attacks.

 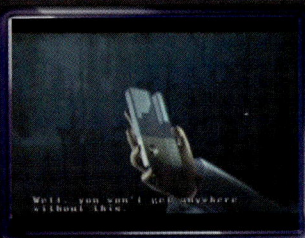

Mr. Freeze has the Asylum staff cold, but he isn't frigid about fighting.

Defeat Mr. Freeze to get this Pass Key from Arkham.

### TAKING DOWN MR. FREEZE
Although high-flying attacks can knock down Mr. Freeze, it's better to get up close and beat him down with lesser attacks that keep him off guard.

# ON TO ZSASZ

Once Mr. Freeze is on ice, Dr. Arkham and his staff are released from their frozen cage. Dr. Arkham doesn't want to give up the Pass Key to the rest of the Asylum, but ultimately relinquishes it. After getting the staff to safety, move outside and use the Pass Key to open the door to the next level of the Asylum. Unfortunately, the next level is populated by even more insane thugs, so beware! Upon entering the door, four enemies appear. Take down each one of them and apply the Batcuffs!

Use the high-security Pass Key to enter the next area of the Asylum.

Move around the corner and enter the room on the left just before the staircase. Smash the crate inside the room to reveal a **Music CD**, then move upstairs to the next room on the left. This room has nothing in it, so continue onward.

Here's another **Music CD**.

Continue down the hallway to the Restricted Area door. Move inside the door, but prepare for a sudden attack! Four inmates stand ready and willing to fight. After subduing all of the inmates, hang a left and go down the hallway to the lone door. There is an inmate and a **Sketchbook** inside a crate in this room. Pick them up and move toward the staircase at the other end of the hallway.

Another tough fight awaits beyond this door.

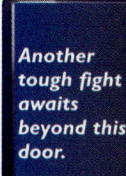

Here's yet another Sketchbook.

89

# ZSASZ

Zsasz has two razor sharp blades. Avoid getting too close to him, or Batman will take some serious damage. It's best to use hit-and-run techniques against Zsasz. Hit him hard, then run away to avoid a counter-attack.

As with Mr. Freeze, try to get close in to Zsasz on occasion and hit him repeatedly with punches or low-level kicks. This should cause significant damage before he can respond. However, this tactic can be dangerous and it's just as likely that he'll shred Batman with his knives. Using a Batarang is another option, but they don't cause much damage.

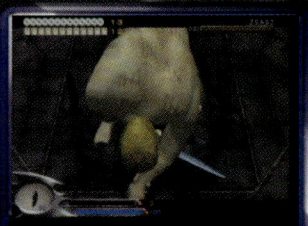

*If you see this, you're in trouble!*

None of the boxes on the narrow staircase on the side of the room contain any items, so don't don't waste any time trying to open them. Likewise, the staircase remains inaccessible until after the fight.

*Back Zsasz up against a wall while punching him and he won't be able to escape.*

After the fight, move up the stairs to find The Joker playing a large pipe organ. It's now time for a show-down against The Joker's men.

# THE JOKER

Joker taunts and baits Batman as his deluded minions—some of the inmates—try to take out Commissioner Gordon, who is tied to a chair in the middle of the room. The inmates will jump down from higher levels to attack the Commissioner. The goal is to stop them before they finish off the Commissioner for good!

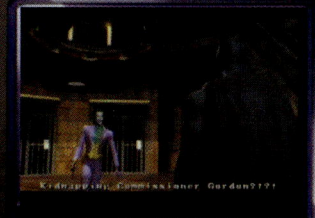 

This fight has three rounds. The first part entails subduing the two inmates on the ground floor. The second part involves running upstairs to the second level of the room. Remember that the enemies will likely jump down and start attacking the Commissioner again. When this happens, jump back down to save him.

The third part involves climbing up to the third level, although the inmates may beat you to it and come down to the Commissioner. Keep an eye on the Commissioner's health bar, because he can only take a few hits before he'll perish. Batcuff all six inmates and victory is at hand!

**Keep the inmate thugs away from the Commissioner!**

**Drats! Rā's al Ghūl is at the root of this nefarious plan!**

# RĀ'S AL GHŪL'S CASTLE

## PART ONE

Commissioner Gordon is now safe, and The Joker is back under the care of Arkham, but The Joker was just a red-herring, and the real culprit who's attempting to destroy the world is Rā's al Ghūl, a man who has lived for hundreds of years. Oracle traces his hideout to the Himalayas in Tibet, which means that you'll be in for a cold spell. To begin with, you'll have to fly (or more accurately, glide) into the area outside Rā's al Ghūl's fortress. After that you'll have to find a way in, and neither is an easy task!

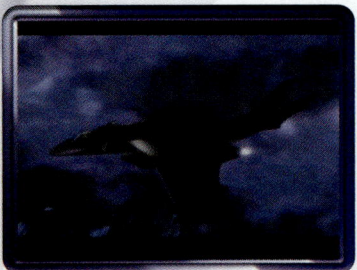

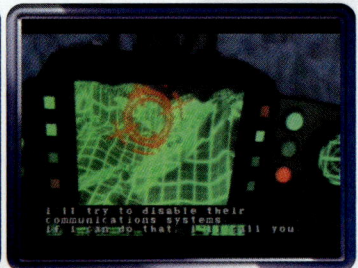

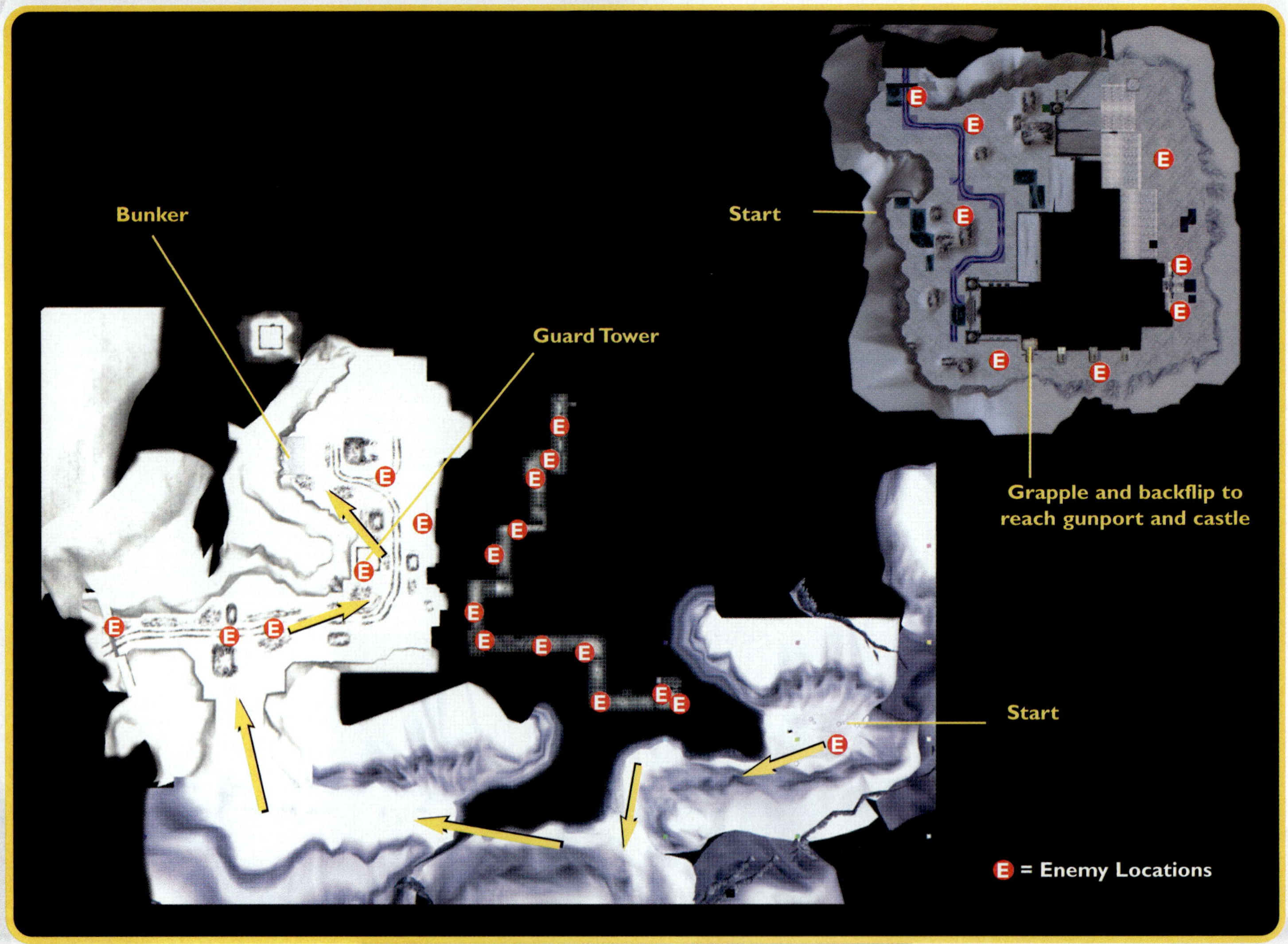

i ll try to disable their
communications systems

Bunker
Start
Guard Tower
Grapple and backflip to reach gunport and castle
Start
E = Enemy Locations

## GETTING INSIDE

# WARNING

Forget about the WAYNETECH crates from this point forward. You won't be able to replenish any items at all (unless you perish and restart).

## FLY BAT, FLY!

After flying the Batjet into the heart of the Himalayas, Oracle reveals a way into the outskirts of Rā's al Ghūl's fortress. The path requires the use of the Batglider. It's not an easy task, though, as the canyon is narrow with treacherous turns. Practice controlling the craft to get accustomed with the controls. Note that the camera view can be switched between first- and third-person perspective. Ultimately, the third-person view provides the most information, but use whichever one you like best.

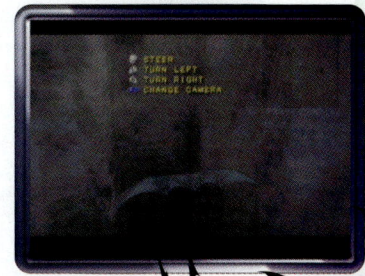
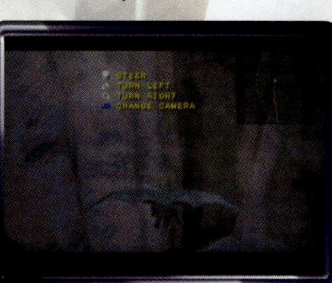

## FLYING THE GLIDER

The Batglider behaves much like a real aircraft. That is, it's possible to enter into a "stall" and end the mission. A "stall" refers to an aerodynamic stall, which means there isn't enough air passing over the glider's wings to provide lift. For this reason, keep a close eye on the glider's speed and don't pull up too much on the glider. Doing so may cause it to stall, thus sending the glider and Batman to an untimely demise.

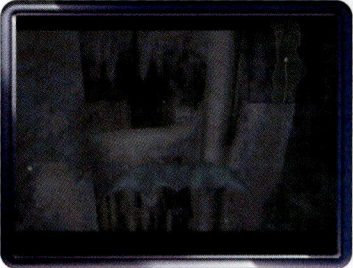

Don't over control the craft when passing over the "bridges"; it's easy to hit them when moving erratically.

Although the canyon has a rather simple look and the darkened conditions make it difficult to see details, there are a few areas that *are* distinct. Eventually, you'll see a "bridge." The glider can't land on it, so you must fly over it. The "window" to fly the glider through is quite narrow, so don't over control the craft.

After clearing the first bridge, the Batglider gets hit with a gust of upward wind that may stall the craft unless preventative measures are taken. To avoid this situation, point the glider's nose down and maintain airspeed. The key is to point the nose down just a little, so that the glider doesn't lose too much altitude. This is key because another "bridge" is fast approaching and it's much higher.

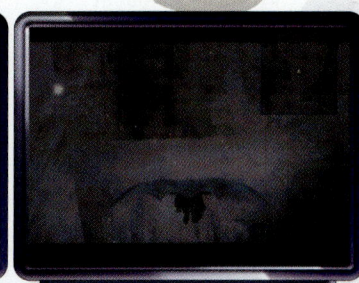

At this point, a gust of wind will push the glider's nose up and slow down the craft.

It's important to gain some altitude to clear the second "bridge."

# RĀ'S AL GHŪL'S CASTLE

After the second bridge comes a very narrow area to fly through. This area has several boulders sticking out from the sides of the canyon, which makes it difficult to judge the distance of the glider to the boulders (especially in third-person view). Therefore, switch to first-person view and simply aim for the opening. After another very tight turn, look for a guard on a ledge below. Wait until the text message appears on-screen, then drop down and take out the guard.

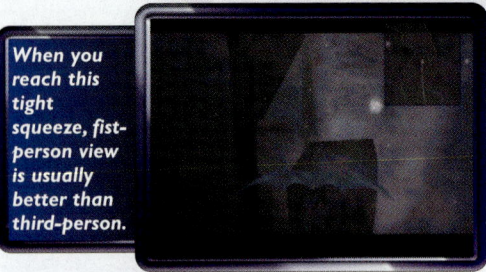
When you reach this tight squeeze, fist-person view is usually better than third-person.

When you see the guard below, drop down.

### BE PATIENT!
This portion of the game is difficult because the area is somewhat dark and there is snow blowing throughout the tight canyon turns. For this reason, it may take several attempts to master this flying aspect of the game. It's very important to keep an eye on the map to see what's coming up.

## PENETRATING THE PERIMETER

Rā's al Ghūl's castle is getting even closer now. First, Batman must traverse a dangerous ledge patrolled by some enemies, then traverse the perimeter defenses of guards and guard towers. The first task is to negotiate a narrow ledge of ice that leads to the guard tower area. Make the appropriate jumps to get through this area, but be wary of the spotlights combing the ground.

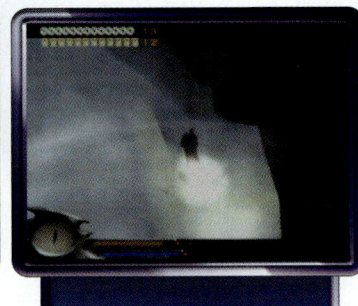
Spotted!

This final jump is a little tricky, so time it up carefully.

## TAKING OUT THE TOWER

You should now be on solid ground. Unfortunately, this area is patrolled by lots of Rā's al Ghūl's guards, including a couple positioned in guard towers. It's possible to gain access to one of the guard towers, so sneak up to it, climb the ladder, and eliminate the guard inside. After doing so, take out the guards on the ground without fear of being sniped at from above.

Take out the other guards after securing the tower.

If you get spotted, run like the wind!

Move to the bunker close to the guard tower. It contains an underground passage that leads to the area just outside Rā's al Ghūl's castle, and it's the only way to get inside.

## THE BUNKER

There are several guards inside the bunker, so be prepared to start fighting right away. Eradicate the guards, Batcuff them, then look around the area. There are two doors to use. One leads to a small room with a fuel drum inside it; blow up the fuel drum to reveal a **Sketchbook**. After doing so, go through the next door with Batarangs at the ready.

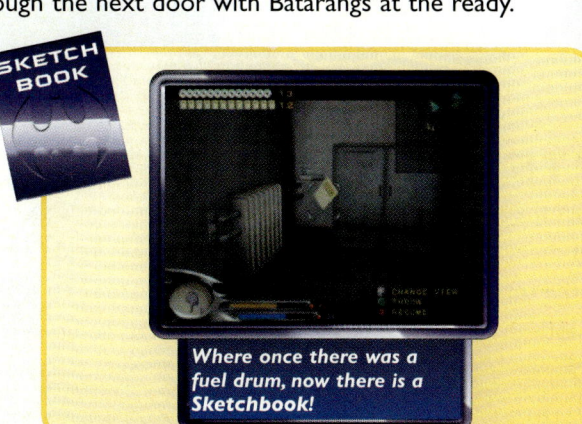

*Where once there was a fuel drum, now there is a Sketchbook!*

The key is to move through the bunker without being detected. This means that you must use Batarangs to take out surveillance cameras. Don't forget to eliminate the guards, too! Continue through the hallways and staircases, taking out each guard who appears. Eventually, the outer courtyard to Rā's al Ghūl's castle will come into view.

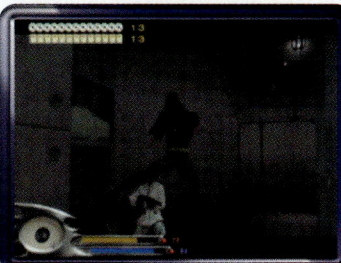

*There's nothing like a good spin-kick to the head to subdue one of Rā's al Ghūl's henchmen.*

### AVOID THE CAMERAS

Notice on the radar the turquoise-colored cones of the enemy video cameras. This indicates the camera's field of vision. If Batman walks into the field of view of one of the cameras, an alarm will sound. Obviously, this makes your task more difficult. To go through unnoticed, throw Batarangs to knock out the cameras.

## OUTSIDE THE CASTLE

The area outside the castle is heavily guarded by at least a dozen guards, several of whom are in gun ports on the side of the castle. Again, attempt to get through the area unnoticed. There are a few guards that *must* be eliminated, but it's not necessary to get into a fighting frenzy with the entire guard force patrolling the castle's perimeter area.

*As shown in the radar, there are plenty of enemies around this area.*

*This is why stealth is important. Once you're spotted, you'll be barraged with ordnance.*

# RĀ'S AL GHŪL'S CASTLE

If the guards are alerted to Batman's presence (and it's likely this will occur), run to the castle door area and disable the guards. Then round the corner to the right to end the aerial bombardment. The side of the castle has several gun ports above. While walking under the first one, you're treated to a top-down view of it. This first gun port is the key to getting into the castle!

*You can take out the guards around the back, but there's nothing of interest there.*

## ENTERING THE CASTLE

Although there are several sets of double doors that look as though they lead into the castle, none of them work so you must find another way inside. Move back to the side of the castle where the top-down view of the gun port appeared. This is where you will enter! Line up underneath the ledge and use the Bat Grapple to go up about two-thirds of the way. Face the wall, then perform a flip to land on the platform!

### WARNING

A spotlight is constantly sweeping over this area. If the guards detect Batman, they'll open fire on him. To avoid detection, grapple and flip onto the ledge. Wait for the spotlight to move past the grappling area, then go to work. When done quickly and efficiently, damage can be avoided altogether.

*This is a tough maneuver, but when done correctly Batman will flip right onto the platform.*

# RĀ'S AL GHŪL'S CASTLE
## PART TWO

This is it! A battle with Rā's al Ghūl. Unfortunately, Rā's al Ghūl has a well-fortified castle that makes things extremely difficult. They key to success in the castle is *stealth!* This point can't be emphasized enough. Avoid detection by the enemies and don't set off any alarms. Some alarms will invariably sound off, but it's important to keep it to a minimum to succeed. The goal is to deactivate the Doomsday Device, then defeat Rā's al Ghūl's guards and ultimately Rā's al Ghūl himself.

### THE DIFFERENT ENDINGS

*Batman: Dark Tomorrow* has several endings. The best ending involves deactivating the doomsday device and defeating Rā's al Ghūl in a sword fight. You can, however, fail to deactivate the doomsday device and still defeat Rā's al Ghūl. This isn't the best of endings, as you're forced to watch millions die on Rā's al Ghūl's video monitors. Finally, you can fail in both endeavors, but let's try to avoid doing that!

**CASTLE COURTYARD**

# RĀ'S AL GHŪL'S CASTLE

Use a stealth approach to eliminate the guards in the castle.

Use a Batarang on this camera to avoid detection.

## THE COURTYARD HALLWAY

Walk through the gun port doorway to access a long hallway that forms a large square. This hallway is on the outer edge of a castle courtyard. First, subdue the guards in the hallways. Move around the entire length of hallway and watch out for guards and cameras.

## THE COURTYARD

There are a couple of ways to get into the courtyard. One is through the door (it's the only unbarred door in the hallway), while the other is through a vent that can be opened with the Universal Tool. Go through the vent to avoid detection early on.

Passing through the vent triggers a cut-scene.

The courtyard is teeming with enemies. Overcoming all of them takes some serious hard work. It's very difficult to use the stealth approach in this situation, so prepare to fight. The doorway is just around the corner from Batman's starting location, but you can't gain access until all of the enemies have been subdued. Start by moving down the archways, taking out each guard as silently as possible!

Use a Batarang to eradicate one of the guards near the fuel drums. After doing so, the other guards come over to investigate. As they approach the fuel drums, toss a Batarang to take them all down en masse!

There are three rows of fuel drums to use while taking out the guards.

### WARNING

Don't get too close to the fuel drums. A stray bullet from a guard's gun will put a serious hurt on Batman's health!

Don't be afraid to use Batman's Batarangs on the guards. Take them all down, then run out and Batcuff them. It's inevitable that some hand-to-hand combat will take place, but it's better than trying to fight them *all* at once. After clearing the front courtyard, move around the back and dispose of two more guards (this is *not* required).

It's not a requirement to take out the two guards around back.

This door leads into the inner castle (Section G).

You're being watched...

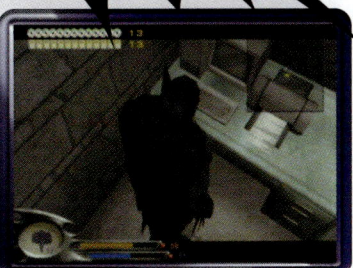

Print out the email from this computer. The email describes the success of the Doomsday Device project.

## SECTION G

Parts of the Castle are divided into sections, specifically sections G, B, D, and C. The first area you enter is Section G, so noted because of the large "G"s painted on the walls. Follow the guard into a room and destroy the three enemies inside. Examine the computer to find an email and print it out.

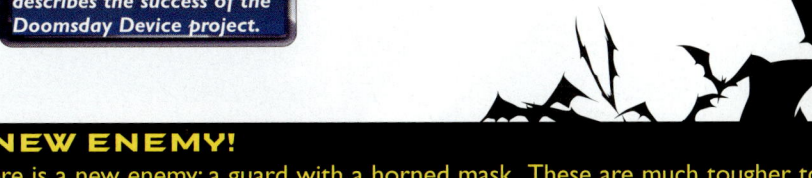

**A NEW ENEMY!**
There is a new enemy: a guard with a horned mask. These are much tougher to defeat and they get up quicker. Don't waste valuable time while Batcuffing them.

The room across the hall contains a truck with the Bat Glider on it. Upon entering the room, four guards descend and initiate combat. Take them out and move to the storage room. Blow up the boxes and fuel drums to find a pair of **Music CDs**.

The last room on the right contains one guard and the third Ammunition Crate. Quietly move in and eradicate the guard, then grab Ammunition Crate #3. After doing so, cross the hallway to the junction room.

There are two Music CDs in this room. Blow up the boxes and fuel drums to find them.

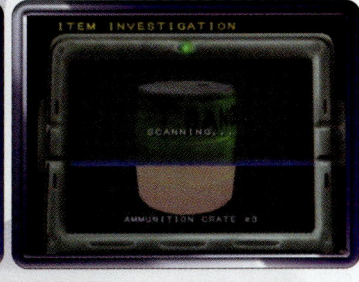

The Ammunition Crate will be scanned after picking it up.

# RÁ'S AL GHÚL'S CASTLE

## THE JUNCTION ROOM

This room is referred to as the junction room because it has five doors, each of which leads to a different area of the castle. There are two doors at the top of the stairs, two doors on the main level, and one door on the far end of the room that is downstairs. Head upstairs and take out the guards patrolling that area, then use a Batarang to destroy the camera.

Move upstairs and defeat the guards.

With the guards down, enter the upper door on the right.

## SECTION D

Guards and cameras watch over section D's long corridors. Use the radar to determine when it's safe to use a Batarang to take out guards or cameras. Continue down the hallway to a door, then enter it. There are several more doors on the other side, but go through the first one. This leads to a sleeping area for the guards. Eliminate the guard in this room, then pick up the **Personal Notes** on the Doomsday Device from one of the bunks.

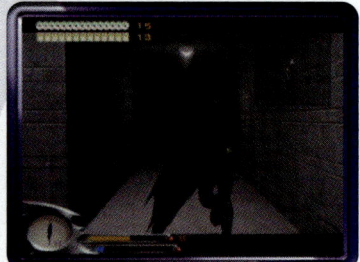   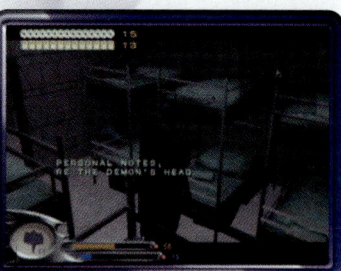

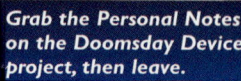
Grab the Personal Notes on the Doomsday Device project, then leave.

There are two more doors in this area. One door leads to another bunk area, while the other one leads to a kitchen area. There is nothing of significance in either area, so return to the junction room.

## JUNCTION ROOM

Back in the junction room, go downstairs and enter the doorway below. This doorway leads to section B.

Take this doorway to section B.

## SECTION B

Subdue the guard in section B. The hallways in this area contain laser trip alarms. To avoid them, jump over them. It's also important to disable the cameras in this area.

 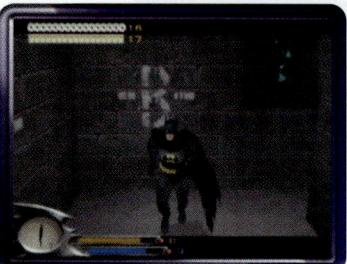 

Jump over the laser trip alarms, and shoot the cameras with a Batarang.

Section B has two doors in it and both are labeled KEEP OUT. The first door (on the left) is locked, so use the Universal Tool to open it. Once inside, subdue the technician. Pick up the notes on the Doomsday Device project, then leave the room. Move to the second door in section B. Once again, use the Universal Tool to open the door. This room has an email on a chair. Pick it up, then return to the junction room.

Get the Personal Notes on the Doomsday Device.

Grab this email.

## JUNCTION ROOM

Go downstairs to the door on the far end. This leads down into the boiler room area where you can grab a few goodies.

## SECTION C (BOILER ROOMS)

There are actually two sets of stairs to descend to get to Section C. Once there, search for two additional doors. It doesn't matter which door you choose, since both doors loop back together! For the sake of this walkthrough, take the door on the left (the one on the open wall). Go to the generator room protected by three guards. There's nothing in this room but a fuel drum. Blow it up to reveal a **Sketchbook**, then continue out the other side of the room.

Take this door.

The next room is the boiler room. Before proceeding inside, smash the crate to reveal a **Music CD**. Inside the boiler room turn the valve until it starts to "whistle," then eliminate the guards. When the coast is clear, return to the Junction Room.

Don't forget this Sketchbook.

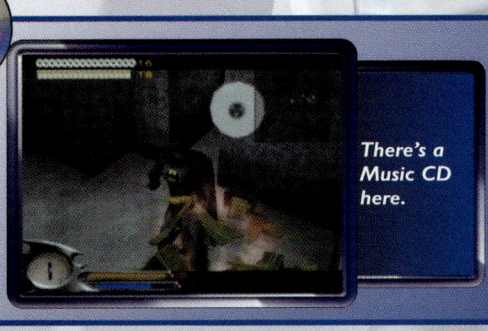

There's a Music CD here.

# RĀ'S AL GHŪL'S CASTLE
## PART THREE

Now that a large portion of the castle has been cleared out, it's time to head to the part of the castle where it all happens—the nerve center!

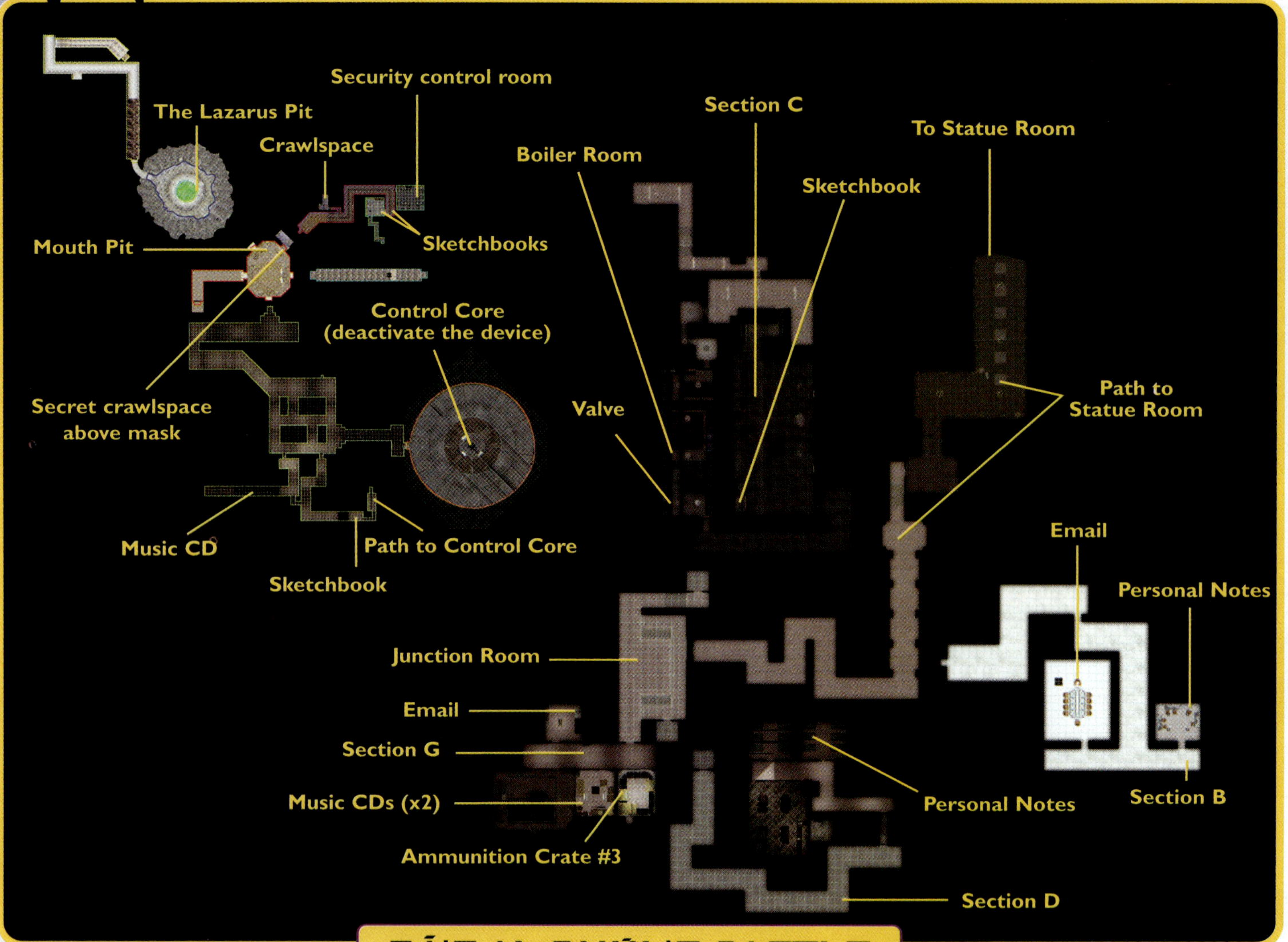

**RĀ'S AL GHŪL'S CASTLE**

Map labels:
- The Lazarus Pit
- Security control room
- Section C
- To Statue Room
- Crawlspace
- Boiler Room
- Sketchbook
- Mouth Pit
- Sketchbooks
- Control Core (deactivate the device)
- Path to Statue Room
- Secret crawlspace above mask
- Valve
- Email
- Personal Notes
- Music CD
- Path to Control Core
- Sketchbook
- Junction Room
- Email
- Section G
- Music CDs (x2)
- Personal Notes
- Section B
- Ammunition Crate #3
- Section D

## JUNCTION ROOM

There is only one door in the junction room yet to explore. This one leads to a room we'll refer to as the Statue Room. It's a large circular room with five faces and open mouths on the walls. Each face (or mouth) leads to a different area. You must travel through each one to deactivate the Doomsday Device *and* defeat Rā's al Ghūl.

*This door leads to the Statue Room.*

## TO THE STATUE ROOM

A series of hallways connect the junction room to the Statue Room. Travel through the hallways, but be on the lookout for cameras and guards.

Continue along until you reach an area guarded by laser traps. As mentioned earlier, jump over the traps to avoid setting them off. Find the large hallway with two guards standing in front of a large set of double doors. Dispose of them with hand-to-hand combat or take them out with Batarangs. Pass through the door to reach the Statue Room.

*Move through this area with stealth and watch for guards and cameras.*

## THE STATUE ROOM

Pass through the large double doors, then move down the hall and into the Statue Room. There are five mouths inside the Statue Room. One leads to the final showdown with Ubu and Rā's al Ghūl, one leads to the Lazarus Pit, one goes to the control area, while the last one leads down to the Doomsday Device control room. For now, take the first mouth to the right.

*There are five mouths to enter, including the one you just came through.*

## DOOMSDAY DEVICE CONTROL AREA

This is where the Doomsday Device (the piece you must deactivate) is located. Go here first to ensure that the alarm system is *not* on when you deactivate the system. If the alarm system has been tripped, you won't be able to achieve this. Move down the hall and dispose of the guard and the camera. After doing so, jump over the laser trap and head downstairs.

 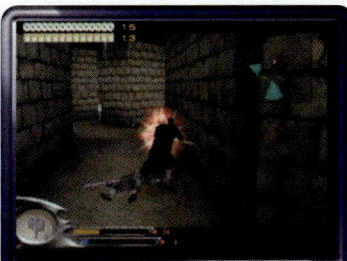

*There are plenty of guards down here.*

### CAN'T SEE ANYTHING?
Use the Night Vision goggles to see where the laser traps are located.

# RĀ'S AL GHŪL'S CASTLE

At the bottom of the stairs, prepare to fight some guards. After subduing them, move to the right and hang the first left up the middle of the room (the room is shaped like a grid). Next, hang a right to find the hallway with two doors (take this path to avoid the laser traps). The first door opens to a large pit, but there's a **Music CD** to pick up; just hit it with a Batarang. Grab the Music CD and go back to the second door.

Use a Batarang to grab this Music CD.

### AVOID DETECTION
It's important to *not* set off the alarms in the control room if you want to deactivate the Doomsday Device. Don't proceed into the control room or attempt anything that may alert the guards. Instead, just follow the suggestions in the walkthrough. After activating the Doomsday Device, do whatever you want.

The second room leads to an area with a large gap. Jump over the gap to reach a **Sketchbook**. More importantly, crouch down and crawl through the vent on the ground. This leads directly to the Doomsday Device control core!

Crouch down to go through the vent.

Jump this gap to access the vent and the Sketchbook.

Follow the vent to the gray room, then move through it to the central control core. Note that there's a flashing red light under the control panel on the core. Move to this area and use the Universal Tool to deactivate the Doomsday Device! After doing so, return to the Statue Room.

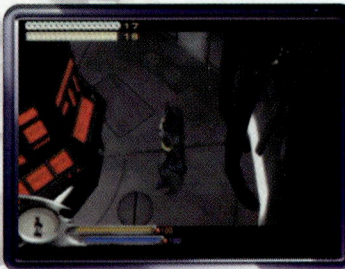

After the computer solves the password problem, the device will be deactivated!

When the panel turns red, leave the area.

### THE UPPER CONTROL ROOM

Although you don't need to go to the upper portion of the control room, you can go down the hallway and into the large circular room and Batcuff the enemies. You cannot, however, deactivate the Doomsday Device by jumping down into the control room. The deactivation can only be accomplished when by approaching the room via the vent.

## STATUE ROOM

The next mouth in the Statue Room leads to the final boss battle, so skip it for now and move to the second mouth on the right. This one leads to the control area (the room with the video monitors). Move through the mouth and take out the guards in the hallway.

*The next mouth to the right leads to the final boss battle, so bypass it for now.*

Use the Universal Tool to open the first door. There are six guards inside manning the surveillance monitors. It's not necessary to go into this room (there are no items inside), but you can do so if you want—just prepare for a difficult fight. When fighting so many thugs in such a tight space, try to take them all down in one fell swoop by using a leg sweep.

*It's a tough fight. Batcuff the thugs once they go down.*

The last door in this area has two **Sketchbooks** in it. Blow up the fuel drum to reveal them. The real surprise is that there's another Sketchbook just above the pipes right outside the door to this room! Collect the Sketchbooks and return to the Statue Room.

*There are two Sketchbooks in this room.*

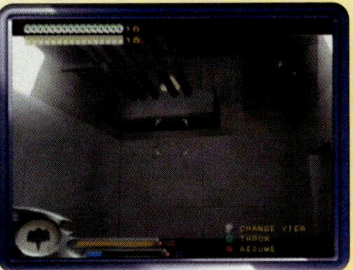

*To find this Sketchbook, crawl on the pipes above, or use a Grapple to shoot at it.*

# RĀ'S AL GHŪL'S CASTLE

Use the Universal Tool to open the gates.

## STATUE ROOM
The last path in the Statue Room leads to the Lazarus Pit. The Lazarus Pit plays a role in the game's finale, but there really isn't anything to do there. Still, if you want to be complete, it's a place you must visit.

## SECRET AREA
Use the Bat Grapple to access the ledge above the face that leads to the control rooms. After smashing a hole in the wall, go to the pipes above the hallway. If you haven't already obtained the **Sketchbook** there, you can do so this way.

## TO RĀ'S AL GHŪL
Return to the Statue Room and go through the mouth that leads to the boss battles. First comes a fight against two Elite Guards, followed by Ubu (Rā's al Ghūl's personal guard), then Rā's al Ghūl! Three battles in a row is tough, but not impossible.

Thus begins the first of three boss fights.

# ELITE GUARDS

The two Elite Guards are both skilled hand-to-hand fighters. The key to defeating them is to ensure that one of the guards is always on the ground! To accomplish this, hit one of the guards right away with a power attack to knock him to the ground. Once he's down, do the same thing to the other guard!

This tactic should create a great opportunity to defeat both guards without taking too much damage. If Batman gets knocked down, the

guards will often move in close. If this occurs, perform a leg sweep counter-attack to take them both down at once! Try to corner one of the guards and continually pummel him with repeated hits until the other guard comes to break things up. After eliminating one of the guards, it's easier to focus on defeating the remaining guard. After the fight, Ubu enters the room and the second fight begins right away!

106

# UBU

Ubu is Rā's al Ghūl's personal body guard and it's his job to ensure that Batman doesn't reach Rā's. Ubu has several attacks. He possesses a standard punch attack that causes a moderate amount of damage. He can also perform a body-slam attack. He sometimes follows this up with a foot-stomp that also inflicts a lot of damage. Lastly, Ubu has a charge attack in which he attacks like a charging rhinoceros! If this attack connects, it will deplete at least one-third of Batman's health!

*Jumping kicks are very effective against Ubu.*

To defeat Ubu, run and hit him with a jumping spin-kick, then run away to avoid a counter-attack. Then run back at him and hit him again. This works for a few reasons, the most important of which is that the constant movement doesn't allow Ubu to set up his charge attack. A Batarang attack is less effective because Batman must stand still to use it. If this occurs, Ubu will likely charge and slam Batman into the wall before the Batarang even releases.

Ubu also has a defensive move that will effectively block attacks. When Ubu puts his arms above his head and crouches down, move away from him and attack later. The hit-and-run tactic works best against Ubu. Hand-to-hand combat just doesn't work.

If you want to return to any portion of Rā's al Ghūl's castle, now is the time to do so. You don't automatically fight Rā's al Ghūl after defeating Ubu, so if there are any items you failed to pick up, now is the time to go back. If not, prepare for the final fight!

# RĀ'S AL GHŪL'S CASTLE

# RĀ'S AL GHŪL

Rā's al Ghūl likes to duel with swords, so this fight is a combination of swordplay and kicking. He's a skilled swordsman with the ability to block attacks. Also, beware of his flurry of sword swipes; getting hit by it will take down nearly half of Batman's health bar. Fortunately, Rā's doesn't use this attack much until the end of the battle.

Quickly rush toward Rā's and start attacking. When he falls, back away to avoid a counter-attack. If he unleashes his stabbing attack, get behind him and hit him while his guard is down. If Rā's blocks the first two or three volleys, then back away because he will likely follow up with a punishing counter-attack. His ability to block attacks is superior, so always try to catch him off guard.

*This fight has fireworks aplenty!*

As the fight progresses he becomes more aggressive with his stabbing attack. In fact, Rā's inflicts most of his damage once his health bar reduces to about one-fourth. Therefore, it's best to have a large Medical Kit (400 health) ready. Don't use a Medical Kit to replenish health; instead, let the kit do it automatically.

When Rā's hit points reach the last 10% or so, quickly move around him, jumping and running all the while. Move in and hit him only when an opening occurs. As mentioned before, Rā's gets much tougher as he gets closer to defeat.

After successfully defeating Rā's, the game ends. But how the game ends depends on whether or not the Doomsday Device was deactivated. If it was, then Rā's and his men have been defeated and the world has been saved. But if not, then Rā's plan to destroy the world becomes a terrifying reality.

*Fail to deactivate the Doomsday Device and you'll see this ending.*

*Successfully deactivate the Doomsday Device and defeat Rā's al Ghūl and you'll see this ending.*

# SECRETS

In *Batman: Dark Tomorrow*, there are numerous Music CDs and Sketchbooks to find. They are usually hidden in out-of-the-way places or inside fuel drums or other objects. It takes thorough exploration and keen use of Batarangs to uncover all of them. The following section provides a brief summary of the location of these items.

To access these goodies, go to the Extras menu and select the music you'd like to play. Or, take a look at some of the cool art that is unlocked in *Batman: Dark Tomorrow*! As an added bonus, the game's various cut-scenes also become unlocked for viewing at any time. Rest assured, the cut-scenes in *Batman: Dark Tomorrow* are very cool!

## QUICK REFERENCE CHARTS

### MUSIC CD AND SKETCHBOOK LOCATIONS

| AREA | MUSIC CDS | SKETCHBOOKS |
|---|---|---|
| Rooftops | 1 | 1 |
| Gotham City Alleyway | 1 | 0 |
| Gazette Square | 1 | 1 |
| Warehouse District | 2 | 1 |
| Gotham Docks | 1 | 2 |
| GCPD Rooftop/Talbot Factory | 1 | 2 |
| Underground Sewers | 2 | 3 |
| Arkham Asylum | 5 | 3 |
| Rā's al Ghūl's Castle | 4 | 5 |

# SECRETS

Some of the artwork that gets unlocked by collecting the Sketchbooks is very cool. Just for fun, here are some of the ones you'll find.

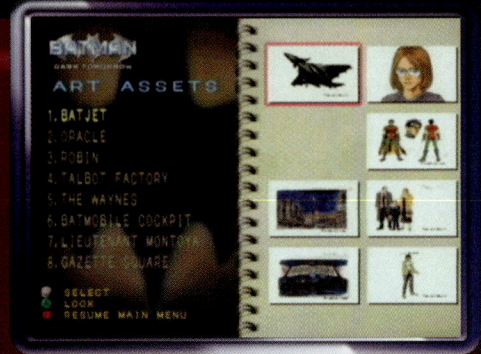

Production Images

Production Images

Production Images

Production Images

## OFFICIAL STRATEGY GUIDE

©2003 Pearson Education

BradyGames is a registered trademark of Pearson Education, Inc.

All rights reserved, including the right of reproduction in whole or in part in any form.

An Imprint of Pearson Education
201 West 103rd Street
Indianapolis, Indiana 46290

Batman: Dark Tomorrow ©2003 DC Comics & Kemco. All rights reserved. All Batman characters and elements are trademarks of DC Comics. All rights reserved. Manufactured and marketed by Kemco.

Please be advised that the ESRB rating icons, "E", "K-A", "T", "M", and "AO" are copyrighted works and certification marks owned by the Interactive Digital Software Association and the Entertainment Software Rating Board and may only be used with their permission and authority. Under no circumstances may the rating icons be self-applied to any product that has not been rated by the ESRB. For information regarding whether a product has been rated by the ESRB, please call the ESRB at (212) 759-0700 or 1-800-771-3772. Please note that ESRB ratings only apply to the content of the game itself and do NOT apply to the content of the books.

**ISBN:** 0-7440-0196-X

**Library of Congress Catalog No.:** 2003101666

**Printing Code:** The rightmost double-digit number is the year of the book's printing; the rightmost single-digit number is the number of the book's printing. For example, 03-1 shows that the first printing of the book occurred in 2003.

06　05　04　03　　　　　　　　　　4　3　2　1

Manufactured in the United States of America.

**Limits of Liability and Disclaimer of Warranty:** THE AUTHOR AND PUBLISHER MAKE NO WARRANTY OF ANY KIND, EXPRESSED OR IMPLIED, WITH REGARD TO THESE PROGRAMS OR THE DOCUMENTATION CONTAINED IN THIS BOOK. THE AUTHOR AND PUBLISHER SPECIFICALLY DISCLAIM ANY WARRANTIES OF MERCHANTABILITY OR FITNESS FOR A PARTICULAR PURPOSE. THE AUTHOR AND PUBLISHER SHALL NOT BE LIABLE IN ANY EVENT FOR INCIDENTAL OR CONSEQUENTIAL DAMAGES IN CONNECTION WITH, OR ARISING OUT OF, THE FURNISHING, PERFORMANCE, OR USE OF THESE PROGRAMS.

## BRADYGAMES STAFF

| | |
|---|---|
| Publisher | David Waybright |
| Editor-In-Chief | H. Leigh Davis |
| Creative Director | Robin Lasek |
| Marketing Manager | Janet Eshenour |
| Licensing Manager | Mike Degler |
| Assistant Marketing Manager | Susie Nieman |

## CREDITS

| | |
|---|---|
| Title Manager | Tim Cox |
| Screenshot Editor | Michael Owen |
| Book Designer | Kurt Owens |
| Production Designers | Tracy Wehmeyer |
| | Tim Amrhein |
| | Christopher Luckenbill |

Batman created by Bob Kane.
Cover painting by Christopher Moeller